Writing to Explore

Writing to Explore

Discovering Adventure in the Research Paper, 3–8

David Somoza & Peter Lourie

Stenhouse Publishers
Portland, Maine

Stenhouse Publishers
www.stenhouse.com

Credits
Pages 14, 32–33, and 87–88: Excerpts from *The Lost Treasure of Captain Kidd* by Peter Lourie. Copyright © 1996 by Peter Lourie. Published by Boyds Mills Press. Reprinted by permission.
Page 44: Excerpt from *The Lost Treasure of the Inca* by Peter Lourie. Copyright © 2002 by Peter Lourie. Published by Boyds Mills Press. Reprinted by permission.

Library of Congress Cataloging-in-Publication Data
Somoza, David, 1967 Dec. 20–
     Writing to explore : discovering adventure in the research paper, 3–8 / David Somoza and Peter Lourie.
        p. cm.
     Includes bibliographical references.
     ISBN 978-1-57110-787-9 (alk. paper)
     1. Report writing. 2. Composition (Language arts) 3. Language arts (Elementary) I. Lourie, Peter, 1952– II. Title.
     LB1047.3.S635 2010
     372.13'0281—dc22
                                                                 2010032036

Cover design, interior design, and typesetting by Martha Drury
Manufactured in the United States of America

PRINTED ON 30% PCW
RECYCLED PAPER

16 15 14 13 12 11 10   9 8 7 6 5 4 3 2 1

Contents

Acknowledgments

Dave:

Thank you to the fifth-grade team at Stevens Elementary (Brett Adams, Betty Hanson, Danielle Seaman, Ellen Sinnenberg, Bev Pineau, Leslie Tasse, Laura VanPatten, Karin Wallimann, and Jon Adams) for your imagination, your wisdom, and your collaborative effort on so many writing projects. Brett, thank you for working with me to develop the adventure writing idea into a dynamic project that motivates and challenges all our students—your ideas are invaluable!

Thank you to Ralph Rothacker, principal of Stevens Elementary, for your continual support and appreciation of our various experiments in the instruction of writing.

Thank you to Dr. Bob Yagelski, professor of education at the University of New York at Albany and coordinator of the Capital District Writing Project, and Carol Formann-Pemberton, high school English teacher and coordinator of the Capital District Writing Project, for your insight and guidance during the summer writing institute and beyond. Your passion for writing inspires us all.

Most of all, thank you to my wonderful students, past and present, who have pushed themselves to become stronger writers and have inspired me in the process.

Dave and Pete:
Thank you to Bill Varner, our wise and humble editor at Stenhouse, for your help and continual encouragement throughout this entire project.

Introduction:
A Passion for Writing

Late one afternoon near the end of the spring semester, I sat in my hot classroom reading through my students' research projects. After months of reading, note taking, and writing, the kids had finally completed their reports on states around the country. They were so excited to have finished their work, and I was excited to read it. But as I read, I became more and more depressed. So much time and effort had gone into creating these master papers, these finished products, these regurgitated encyclopedias. Yeah, that's really what they were. The kids had basically rewritten the encyclopedia in their own words, leaving out some of the details. And the more I thought about it, the more I realized that they hadn't done anything wrong—in fact, they had done exactly what I had asked them to do.

I took a break from reading, got a sip from the hallway drinking fountain, and tried to think of how I had failed so miserably. Returning to the classroom, I noticed Pete Lourie's book *Rio Grande* on the bookshelf. I picked it up, hoping to procrastinate a little longer. As I began to read through it, I realized that this was exactly what I had hoped to find in my students' projects: interesting and engaging nonfiction, factual writing with an emotional center—in short, an *adventure*. As I sat there reading, I decided

1

that I had to teach my kids to do this. I called Pete, a friend for many years, and told him about my frustrating afternoon and the hope that his Rio Grande book had given me. He sounded surprised that I was surprised that nonfiction could be so interesting. We talked for a long time, and have talked many hours since then over the years, about how to teach students to write really interesting adventure stories based in nonfiction. The more I learned about Pete's process for writing adventure stories, the more fascinated I became with the idea of replicating this process with my students in the classroom.

Once I began to experiment with this idea, I had some great results. Pete also became more and more interested in what I was doing. Students were now conducting research online and using it as a basis to develop stories rooted in real places, supported by facts and developed with detailed descriptions of images from real locations. The model I had chosen came from the genre of adventure writing, and seemed perfect for our project: history and geography were woven together to make these adventure-based papers complete. Meanwhile, Pete embarked on more adventures around the world, which he worked into his books and discussed with me.

The more Pete and I talked, the more we realized that we had a lot in common in our approach to writing and teaching. We realized, too, that adventure writing was a genre that worked remarkably well with students. As a departure from the traditional research paper, this approach would involve student research but would integrate it with aspects of the craft of fiction writing. The process promised to be more engaging, more personally relevant, and more rewarding for students. The products would represent not only their research but also their self-expression through imaginative writing.

So our goal in this book is really twofold. We want to break down the barrier between the "real world" (the adventurous world "out there") and the world of the classroom by showing how teachers and professional writers can learn from one another to establish a learning environment that is as real as it gets. Perhaps more important, we want to demonstrate how to use the adventure writing model as an effective solution to the multiple dilemmas faced by writing teachers and social studies teachers every day, especially when it comes to the often dreaded research paper. The process of creating this book has been challenging and amazingly rewarding. We hope you will find it equally inspiring and informative—in short, a great adventure.

A little background. As a kid I never liked writing much. No, that's not true—I hated writing. It was such a laborious task, and I could never get it right. My handwriting was unreadable, and it seemed that the assigned subject was always dull and artificial. To me, writing was a contrived way of wasting time, with no link to what was real in the world. My mind was always racing off to some faraway place—anywhere outside of class, really—only to be dragged back to the drudgery of completing some random writing task. And I could never just do it to get it over with. It was always a painful process, like pulling my hair out one strand at a time.

My dad was, and still is, a great writer, so I knew that writing could be a beautiful thing. But the way that writing was taught in school was altogether different from the way that my dad experienced it. For him, writing was a way of exploring new ideas, traveling in his own mind and finding some sense of understanding. It was a fulfilling experience that had a positive and profound impact on his life. The passion for writing that I saw in him was nowhere to be found in my elementary classroom experience.

As I got older I learned how to do the basics to get by. I wrote the required essays, with much pain but no emotion. And so I finally learned how to write; but instead of trying to find a way to make my writing connect with anything in my life, I decided that writing was an abstract chore that simply had to be done, like brushing your teeth. It wasn't until after college that I began to really enjoy writing for its own sake.

After finishing my degree in architecture, I was hired by a large architecture firm in Albuquerque and worked eighty-hour weeks. This intense schedule made life a blur, and I needed to find a bit of time for myself. Strangely, I found it through writing. Each morning I arrived early at the office, put on some music, and just wrote until the rest of my coworkers arrived. Sometimes I jotted down memories, sometimes dreams from the night before, sometimes just images described in detail. This soon turned into a habit that became rather obsessive at times. Even if I couldn't remember every detail of a dream, or if I couldn't get the words just right, it didn't matter. I wrote because it was fun to get the ideas out. I never bought a journal or even used full sheets of paper. It was more fun to scribble on sticky notes or yellow trace paper. Eventually I took my scraps of paper home and even typed a few of them up. But most of them were useless, just bits of images that had seemed really important to me in the mornings before work.

It wasn't until several years later that I decided to give up architecture and go back to school to study education. Years later, I realized the value of my writing these bits of images and dreams during those early hours at the office. I had found a way to explore new ideas and better understand my thoughts, which no other medium, not even drawing, could provide for me. Writing had lifted me out of the humdrum of a hectic workplace and taken me to places I might have daydreamed about as a kid back in elementary school.

Now, it's been sixteen years since I began teaching fifth graders, and I love it more than ever. But of all the things I teach, I find writing the most difficult *and* the most enjoyable.

When I began my first teaching assignment in Colorado, I quickly came to realize that a large part of teaching elementary school is taken up with the task of writing. But I didn't know how to teach writing in a way that was different from the way I was taught. It began as a series of disasters that over time grew slightly less disastrous, until eventually things started to fall into place piece by piece. My biggest goal and greatest obstacle was finding a way for my students to love writing. With a great deal of experimentation and through much trial and error I've found a few ways to make this happen. The most rewarding of all has come by way of adventure writing, which engages students in the writing process while expanding their understanding of the many complex aspects of the craft. Adventure writing appeals to kids because they can imagine it. It's not abstract—it's real, and it's exciting.

As Bilbo used to say, "It's a dangerous business, Frodo, going out your door . . . You step onto the Road, and if you don't keep your feet, there is no knowing where you might be swept off to."

—J. R. R. Tolkien, *The Fellowship of the Ring*

Step One

Building Blocks

Chapter 1

Setting Descriptions

In the fall of my first year, I wanted to get my students excited about writing, just as it had become for me. The problem was I didn't have a clue how to make this happen. I also had weird notions about teaching, that there were certain things that all teachers taught and that teaching was supposed to be done in some prescribed way. I had my students begin by writing sentences and paragraphs, and I focused on all the important composition and grammar techniques, but that was not inspiring anyone, especially me.

Being the clueless new teacher that I was and having failed at my first attempts as a writing teacher, I decided that my only real option was to experiment trial-and-error style. My students needed creative writing experiences—maybe like the ones I had created for myself after college at the architecture firm. I decided that first they must fall in love with writing, and only after that (if ever) could I interest them in mechanics.

Not wanting to limit their creativity, I had them write stories. "About what?" they asked. "About whatever really interests you," I said earnestly. Wow, what a flop that was. Some kids sat there looking bored, others were annoyed, most were nervous. Often kids began with, "Hi my name's Sally and I'm going to tell you all about my cocker spaniel, ok?"

So I tried to narrow the focus a bit. "Try to write about a dream that you've had," I said.

"But I don't remember my dreams," was the common reply.

"Make one up."

"OK! Hi my name's Sally and I'm going to tell you . . ."

Then I hit upon what I thought was a novel idea, an early and yet unformed version of the adventure essay. "All kids love adventure stories," I said to myself. "OK, kids, today we're going to write adventure stories. Let's make 'em really exciting!" That was a flop too, maybe the biggest flop of all. I got a bunch of comic-strip stories—all action but no substance. They wrote stories about subjects they knew nothing about, so they weren't convincing. These essays may have been fun to write, but they were painful to read. Every sentence except the first one started with "then," and they always ended with the main character dying. The setting was never described, so you couldn't picture the scene; and when the main character died, you didn't really care, because throughout the entire story you never really got to know anything more about him than his name.

My trial-and-error approach to teaching writing had been exactly that—trial and error, with an emphasis on the error. I decided that to get good writing I had to do a bit more work. I realized that many of my kids still had no interest in writing. And as badly as the other kids wanted to write good stories, they just didn't have the skills or the experience. "Let's start with the setting," I thought. "Then we can work on character development, story elements, and all the other good stuff, and then we'll put it all together and create great stories."

I looked through books to find interesting scenes that were written well enough and with enough detail for the reader to clearly imagine them. One of my favorites came from the opening scene of *Bless Me, Ultima*, which draws you in: ". . . the raw, sun-baked llano, the green river valley, and the blue bowl which was the white sun's home. My bare feet felt the throbbing earth and my body trembled with excitement. Time stood still, and it shared with me all that had been, and all that was to come . . ." (Anaya 1999, 1). I can still picture standing there barefoot on that eastern slope of the northern New Mexico mountains, that harsh environment where plains and mountains meet.

After reading through many scenes in books, I realized that readers don't get attached to a setting unless they can imagine themselves there, and I noticed that a lot of great stories began with a descriptive scene. You need to be planted in the place and see what's around you, feel the cool morning breeze on your bare arms, smell the pine scent and last night's campfire lingering in the air, hear the swishing of the wind in the tops of the fir trees. And when you look down, you have to see your boots, covered in dirt and ash, rooted in the soft, powdery sand.

Light is another important feature of a descriptive setting; it lets you know what time of day it is, brings color to the picture, and illuminates specific parts of the scene. Light brings changes to the scene, too, and influences the mood, as when the sun breaks through clouds, glows in all its colorful glory at the end of the day, and turns oranges to purples as it settles deep beyond the horizon. Our senses make a place memorable, and that's what I wanted to read in my kids' writing.

I talked about this with Pete to see how he felt about the importance of setting in his writing. His response let me know that I was moving in the right direction:

> **When I travel to work on a book, I'm drawn into stories through the simple act of being in a particular place. Hearing the roar of howlers and the whine of cicadas in the long, hot jungle afternoons in Chiapas, Mexico, for example, is an important part of my research into the ancient Maya civilization. This is the starting point where the mystery can come alive. First and foremost for me, it's all about where I am and, by inference, where the reader is. Readers should feel, hear, and smell what I felt, heard, and smelled. Every place is different in specific ways. Those specifics are what I try to capture in my writing.**
>
> **Some writers are more adept at capturing the nuance of character; others do better with action and plot; some specialize in internal monologue. Me? Nothing can happen until I reach a place. I love creating in the minds and hearts of a reader a certain setting. It's the feel of a place that makes me the happiest or the most frightened—the sounds, the smells, the light on a leaf. The setting of my stories makes it possible to write anything at all. Places—jungles, mountains, rivers, or simply a hot, humid day in late August in my writing cabin. From the smells and sights and sounds of a place I launch into an investigation of story, history, plot, and character. Place is the ground on which the architecture of stories is created.**

So I looked through my cabinets at school and found some old Sierra Club nature calendars, dismantled them, and laminated the pictures. In class the next day we began with a brainstorming session where we used detailed descriptions to define a setting, any setting. I made a big chart on the board where we listed ordinary ways to describe a setting and then tried to come up with more creative ways. We threw out words like "pretty" and "nice" and all the general ones that tell us nothing and replaced them with specific words like "shimmering" and "rough-textured." Through our discussion several kids came up with similes, so we talked about the use of similes and metaphors as great tools to empower our writing. That led to a discussion about the use of multisensory language. Can you smell this picture? Feel the breeze from that picture? Hear the crashing waves in the background of those? What does it smell like? Feel like? Sound like?

The experiment worked. And that's where their writing took off. The kids loved the exercise, and they wrote with passion. When a kid said he was finished, I suggested that he try using other senses, that he describe a yet undiscovered set of details in the photos—plants, light, a mountain peak, a pattern in the sand, whatever. They found that they could keep going back and finding more to write about each time. One kid jumped up and grabbed a magnifying lens from the science table and searched for minute details in the crevices of rocks. This was the most excitement I'd ever seen in writing class, and their essays were wonderful. It was the first writing exercise that I felt really good about because the kids were tapping into their own creativity, and each one produced something that was truly unique.

One morning when the pieces were finished and polished, the kids came in to find all their calendar pictures pinned up on the board. I read the first piece aloud without mentioning the author's name. Then I had the kids try to guess which photo had just been described. There was a bit of discussion, but we narrowed it down to three or four possibilities. I read it again, and it was clear. It had to be the one in the bottom right-hand corner. "Would the author please stand up and tell us if we're right?" I asked. Jon, who had been trying to keep his excitement inside, stood up, beaming from ear to ear. "You're right!" he yelled. We continued this game and found that after one or two readings we could always identify the right image. I ended the session by reading a very general essay I had written, something like, "I'm in a beautiful place in nature. Everything I see is so pretty, and it smells wonderful . . ."

The kids quickly saw that this could be any of the photos. I had made my point and the kids could see the value of using descriptive language. We talked about the importance of carefully defining a scene so that the reader can clearly see what the writer could see when he was writing it. I think it sank in. And for those who reverted back to general language after that, I could just remind them of this activity as a reference point. I would say, "Look at this description that you wrote at the beginning of the year. I know you can write with your senses; I know you can write with details."

The main thing I learned from this experience is that kids, all kids, are incredibly imaginative, and that it's our inability to tap into their imagination that results in poor writing, not that kids don't have anything imaginative to say.

When asked to describe an idyllic ocean scene, ten-year-old Colin wrote:

I can see out almost forever. A soft breeze blows across my face, and the cool white sand runs through my toes like sugar coating the ground. The air smells of salt. On the sea, there are waves of thunder crashing up against the shore. The sky is a giant rainbow starting from the bottom up. The afternoon sun makes the grasses look like gold, and the sand bar stretches its sandy arms out about a mile. This is anyone's paradise.

Other fifth graders did an equally remarkable job of using their imaginations to take them into and beyond the scenes of their calendar photographs. Klara looked deeply into her photograph and pulled out tiny details that help us imagine a scene for ourselves when she described a grove of cacti as being "tall and pointed, sea green, and some seem to have grown arms out of their spiky green bodies." She located distant rock cliffs and found that they, "support plant life, coloring parts of them moss green."

Similarly, Marion zoomed in on a patch of desert flowers and used her imagination to describe how "their fragrance hangs in the air, and every time I inhale I smell their sweet scent. I bend over and sniff a white flower with a yellow center of small stalks bearing pollen. Its petals feel like butter."

In detailing a mountain pond, Matt selected precise words to paint the scene with "cold, emerald blades of grass around the pond stand microscopic in the shadow of the huge mountains."

Looking back on this activity, I see that it did more for my students than teach them how to describe a landscape; it opened their eyes to the reality that they had untapped talent.

At the beginning of each year the most reluctant writers will come into my class with a mixture of apathy and disgust for writing. This activity, however, is so concrete and clear and yet so open to individual creativity at the same time that everyone succeeds. Their success is public; and everyone in the class claps as each piece is read.

Take Robert, for example. He hated to write anything, even notes off the board. He was a minimalist in his writing, and even abbreviated his name at the top of his papers. He had no interest in doing this writing and no reason to believe that he was remotely capable of doing a decent job. He sat there, staring at the picture. "What do you see?" I asked.

"A big empty desert!"

"Good, write that down. Is it totally empty?"

"There's mountains in the back."

"Great! What color are they?"

And pretty soon he was ready for a bit of a leap. "How do you think the air would feel if you were standing right there in that picture?"

So it's not something that everyone can initially do independently, but with a few short prompts and pertinent questions to get some of the kids going, they can take off on their own fairly quickly. Robert got stuck a few times along the road and needed this sort of quick help to get him refocused. In the end, though, when his piece was finished, it was all his, and he worked hard to hold back his smile.

I find that it's also helpful to give the kids samples of what I'm talking about. Show them how writers define their settings so vividly that readers can clearly imagine themselves there, like in this scene from Pete's *The Lost Treasure of Captain Kidd*:

We paddled like crazy. As we came by the western shore of the island, the canoe dipped and rose in the waves like a cork. Faintly I saw the castle wall above us reaching high into the pressing fog. The brick face vanished into mist. Then the fog dropped suddenly and swallowed the wall.

That's when we heard it. Somewhere from inside that fog. A screech, a shriek, a scream. I cannot describe it. But it came from the other side of the island, an inhuman sound cutting through the fog that no living creature ever could make. The unearthly shriek reverberated off the fog as if in some diabolical echo chamber.

Killian instantly pointed the canoe downriver toward Cold Spring. In our escape we were a perfect paddling team, stroking fast, hard, and absolutely in unison.

Into the oncoming waves we paddled for our lives. But the cry, or whatever it was, came only once. We didn't hang around to see if it would come again. (Lourie 2000a, 31)

This year my friend and colleague Danielle Seaman tried this project with her class. Initially she found that her students had trouble coming up with sensory descriptors (other than sight) when looking at the calendar pictures in the classroom. My students often struggle with this at first too, but she had a great idea, which I had never thought to try. She took her class outside to sit on a hill behind the school. As they sat there, they tried describing their surroundings in great detail. She had them describe the smell of the pine trees and newly cut grass, the sounds of the birds in the trees, and the feeling of the warm moist breeze on their arms. When they returned to the classroom they were much better able to imagine all of the senses that they would experience in the calendar images on their desks. This simple exercise opened a door for her students and allowed them to tap into their powers of observation. I look forward to trying this with my own students.

Here are a few more setting essays in their entirety. In each example the writer uses details and sensory descriptors to draw readers into the scene and experience it for themselves.

In this first essay, Aubrey brings the wintery image to life with details like the smells of "pine and forgotten wood," "a slight breeze whistling through the trees," and the sense that "somewhere underneath [her] there are animals hibernating."

Winter Canyon
by Aubrey

(Based on a photograph of the Grand Canyon's rim in winter)

While I sit here, watching, waiting I hope for something interesting to happen. I look out and see a beautiful canyon covered with a thin layer of shining snow. It looks perfect for winter fun, like sledding. I look around me and see more wonderful snow. I reach out to feel it and it seems soft as a pillow that someone like me could lay down and fall asleep in.

A slow fog is forming and the air smells strongly of pine and forgotten wood. A slight breeze whistling through the trees is what I hear. I stand up and start to weave under and over the fallen trees, not minding the scratchy feeling of brown bark and the prickly feeling of dark, green pine as I pass. I know that somewhere underneath me there are animals hibernating.

I look up towards the sky. It has become dim and I know I should be getting home. I say goodbye to this world of cold, yet wonderful snow as I imagine a warm toasty fire back at home.

Maybe tomorrow I will walk along this rocky ledge and explore what lies beyond my eyes. I could explore that creek in the canyon too! I glance back at the canyon and imagine it will be as spectacular, historic, and beautiful as the Grand Canyon. As I start off towards home, I hope that someday I will visit Winter Canyon again.

Megan, with her attention to detail, finds just the right words to create moving images in my mind as I read her essay. I can clearly picture the "silver minnows [as they] dart about in the water like silver arrows" and the white sand from the shore as it "comes up and is carried a little ways by the current and then settles down again."

A Summer Day with the Mountains
by Megan

(Based on a photograph of a high mountain lake in summer)

A bee buzzes around my head before seating itself on a flower to feed on its sweet nectar. It is a clear sunny day and I am standing in a field of pretty pink flowers. The flowers have a strong sweet-smelling fragrance and I can faintly smell the pine forest from across the lake. A long, moss-covered bolder that looks like a bench overlooks the clear, blue lake. It is such a hot day and I decide to walk down to the lake to start wading. The water is cold and has no trace of sediment. My throat is telling me to take a sip of water from the lake.

The mountains have patches of grass on them and small deserts of sand. The bare tops of the mountains are easy to see against the blue sky and look very pretty. I can see the highest points of the mountains starting to get lost in the fog.

There are small, young maple trees mixed into the flowers. I think that someday the field of flowers might be a maple forest like the pine forest across the lake.

I bend over to take a sip of water from the lake. The water is cool, sweet and refreshing, like lemonade. I watch silver minnows dart about in the water like silver arrows. I wiggle my toes in the pure white sand at the bottom. White sand comes up and is carried a little ways by the current and then settles down again. I start to wade towards the rolling mountains, seeing how they all look like people standing in a line. Slowly I climb onto a grassy bank to dry off, listening to the waves lapping against the shore, thinking what a peaceful place this is.

Eva, too, captures the nuances of the scene with fresh words to describe more than just the obvious. Beyond the flowers, she shows how "their dark shadows are scattered in the golden sand," and she finds just the right words to paint an image with "a line of animal tracks trailing in the ripples." It's these precise and carefully crafted details that take a generic scene and make it really come alive for the reader.

The Peaceful Desert
by Eva

(Based on a photograph of a desert scene in New Mexico)

It is a bright sunny day as I walk in the golden rippled sand. In the distance I can see rocky mountains lined up like soldiers. The mountains are brown, but in some places it is darker than other places, from the sun. In front of the mountains, are patches of grass everywhere. The grass is dried up and a light brown from the sun. The grass lies flat, covering the sand like a blanket. There are little bushes of grass scattered in the blanket. When I look up in the sky, it looks like somebody painted white streaks in the blue. The sky is a faded blue, with the white colliding into it.

I sit down in a nice cool spot in the sand next to a single yellow flower. Its big green leaves stick out of the stem, with one buried beneath the sand. A little farther off are bunches of purple and white flowers in green tangled vines. A few of the purple petals are buried beneath the sand, with the purple color visible in the sand. Their dark shadows are scattered in the golden sand. There is a line of animal tracks trailing in the ripples.

I slip off my shoes; the grains of sand feel cool between my toes. I close my eyes. After a while I open them once again, and slip my shoes back on. A small breeze blows the loose hair from my ponytail around for a little while.

I get up and continue to walk—next to the animal tracks, past the flowers, into the grass, and towards the mountains.

Teaching Tips

Images: I find that any rich, nature photograph will work well for this activity. I like calendars because they're beautiful and cost-effective. Buy them after January and you can get them for next to nothing. Laminate them for extended use.

Brainstorming: Start with the senses and have the kids supply you with lists of descriptions involving different senses. Distinguish between general and specific descriptions. Have your students try to find more specific descriptions. You can take them through a series of steps, making the descriptions more and more specific as you go.

Metaphor and Simile: This is a great time to introduce metaphor and simile as tools to enrich descriptions.

Background and Foreground: Introduce background and foreground and vocabulary that can help the reader "walk" their way through the descriptions.

Getting Started: Students will often mention the obvious first. Since sight is the only sense available to you from a photo, have the kids use their imaginations to fill in the rest. Get them to take it to the next level by asking them questions. Can you feel the breeze? How does the sand feel beneath your feet? How do the waves sound as they crash and then recede? What does the air smell like?

Presentation: Hang up all the photographs and read the final essays aloud. This turns the activity into a game where the kids have to determine which photograph is being described in each essay. To make it easier to name a photograph, I hang the photos in a grid and label each column with a letter and each row with a number, so students can say, "I think it's D-7." When the correct photo is identified, have students try to determine which pieces of precise language helped in its identification.

Chapter

Writing Atmosphere

Once I was able to get my kids into writing, I started to write along with them. This was a great learning experience for me, for a few reasons. I realized pretty quickly that some of the ideas for writing activities that sounded good to me in theory were really tough to do in actuality. Sometimes an idea was just terrible and had to be thrown out. Other times it was just a matter of tweaking the idea a bit or giving the kids more information to turn a frustrating lesson into a successful one.

The most important thing I learned by writing with my kids is that the environment in which they write really matters. From my background in architecture, I knew a bit about how to manipulate the mood of a space through the use of light, building materials, textures, proportions, and so on. But it wasn't until I started writing with the kids that I saw what an impact those factors could have on the classroom.

The first thing I noticed was the lighting. I had a tough time writing in the flickering, bright blue, fluorescent glow. It made the lines on my paper swim and constantly distracted my attention. I remember sitting there and looking around at my kids, who were writing away, and thinking, "How do they do this?" It drove me nuts. Along with the visual annoyance came the persistent buzzing of the fluorescent lights. You don't notice it most of the time, but when it's silent and you're trying to write, it suddenly becomes loud and distracting.

I noticed something else about light and writing. In a bright room it's hard to imagine being elsewhere. Maybe your writing is set in a forest, maybe you're walking down a city street, maybe you're at a café at night, but you certainly aren't in a classroom. As I wrote with my kids, the brightness kept bringing me back to the fact that I was in a classroom, and it was difficult to imagine being elsewhere in my writing.

Anything is better than fluorescent lights. Opening up the blinds and turning off the lights immediately makes it a more inviting place to write. Not only does this fix the light and sound problems, but it changes the mood. I noticed that I felt more secluded with less light, and this was a good thing. With the blaring overhead lights the kids are peeking over at your notebook, and you're peeking over at theirs. But with less light you can be more alone, more private, and become more immersed in your writing. In a few years they may be half blind from writing in the dark, but at least they'll be great writers.

I like lamps, too. Often I close the blinds, turn off the overheads, and turn on a few desk lamps. This changes the mood dramatically and is even more inviting to writing, in my opinion. The yellowish light of incandescent bulbs is warmer than fluorescents, more like a fire. It seems to help create a better atmosphere for kids to write in. Why are ceilings so high in classrooms? Maybe it's to fly paper airplanes. I think high ceilings make the space less intimate and less conducive to writing. Lamps have the ability to draw the ceiling down by condensing the height of the space to that which is illuminated. Just a few cheap desk lamps with nice shades work great to create a peaceful atmosphere in the room. One year my fifth graders and I were studying structures in science. We built a large-scale suspension bridge and a tower out of wood and cables. When we finished, one of my students suggested that we turn them into lamps to use during writing. So we figured out a way to work unconventional but effective lampshades into the designs. Then we ran wires through them and used them as lamps. For years they've lit my room. Unfortunately, the fire marshal didn't think they were as cool as I did, so they're now in my basement—time to get out the old desk lamps again. Getting away from fluorescents is key.

Writing with my kids also taught me that it's important to get a handle on the sounds in the room. Once the kids are deep into their writing, they're in a completely different place in their minds. It's crucial that we allow them to stay in that stream of consciousness. I have found that I can be writing away and get yanked back to the classroom by the sudden sound of a pencil sharpener, a kid talking, or an announcement on the intercom. Well, I know I can't do much about the intercom, but I can control the rest. That's why I establish a set of guidelines for writing time. I'm actually kind of militant about it, but the kids understand why it's important and buy into it. During writing time no one goes to the bathroom, no one sharpens a pencil, and no one talks to a neighbor. If I have to talk to a kid, I always whisper and move slowly, so as not to distract the others. I give everyone a few minutes before writing to sharpen pencils, go to the bathroom, and ask any questions.

Music is another great way to manipulate the classroom environment. For one thing, it blocks out any small, distracting noises in the room. But in addition it can really help kids take off to another world in their minds as they write. Over the years I've experimented with all different types of music and have found that certain types are more effective for my students in certain conditions than others. I'll talk more about music later, but I think that music and lighting are two key elements in creating atmosphere.

I had some ideas of my own about writing atmosphere, but I wanted to know what Pete had to say. I suspected that atmosphere would be pretty important to him, too.

Writers are divided on the issue of where they write and what "atmosphere" has to exist for them to produce. Some say it shouldn't or doesn't matter. The act of writing, these few say, is separate from outside influences. Others have to be in their cabins at a certain time of day. Most writers I know have developed some kind of ritual that works for them.

At the very least writers agree that regularity is a must for the job of writing, not unlike an office worker who gets to work at nine, breaks for lunch at twelve for an hour, and then punches out at five. Following regular patterns, writers find they work best when they are sitting at their local library, in their cabins or special rooms, or wherever, but every day and at the same time, cup of tea or coffee in hand. Writing is helped by following rituals and routines. One novelist enters the mood of her stories by reading passages of the Bible before she begins her day; another plays Bach's *Goldberg Variations*; another has two cups of coffee and kneels to the sun rising in the east. Most just dive into the creative waters at prescribed times of day.

The main goal of the writer at the outset is to find a pattern that suits him or her. For me, it's six a.m. in a cabin on a seemingly abandoned lake in the Adirondack Mountains of northern New York State, where eagles have built their nests over my roof.

The routine? I arrive at ten p.m. the night before my work begins, with a carload of books, computer and printer, notes and notebooks, audiotapes that hold my journals from various trips around the world, and five days' worth of food supplies so I won't have to break the spell of solitude to go to town and fritter away the hours shopping for something I forgot to bring.

At precisely six a.m. on the first morning I sit at the dining room table with all my books and notes around me. The phone does not ring, but the wings of the eagles landing in their nest above me sometimes startle me out of my concentration. In the fall the leaves turn and drop, in the winter the snow floats like feathers in the frozen, indigo air. Coffee helps. Long periods of quiet help. The crystal spell of the north-country wilderness improves my focus hour after hour.

When I need to work at home in Middlebury, Vermont, I often write at the college library surrounded by undergraduates. Even there I can find this north-country peace. Focus, after all, is the ultimate goal of all the rituals and routines. In the end it's not really the place as much as the attention to routine. I take the cabin with me in my heart. No matter where I roam, my writing center is that desk in front of the sliders looking out on the lake.

It was helpful to get Peter's perspective as a writer who thinks about the writing atmosphere every day. It also confirmed my own thoughts about the importance of atmosphere and routine. In the classroom, there are more limitations, but it's still possible to create an environment that allows kids to feel uninhibited during the creative process. Developing some guidelines helps maintain this writing environment.

For example, when I first started teaching I let the kids ask me questions during these quiet writing times. Usually the questions were either "How do you spell _____?" or "Is this good?" I would help kids with their spelling or say, "Yes, that's good." But after a while I realized that the more I helped kids with spelling and grammar, the more they focused on it. I don't think it's bad for them to want to use correct spelling and grammar, but it seems to me that grammar and imagination aren't very compatible. So now I tell the kids, "When you're in the creative process of writing, don't worry about spelling, don't worry about grammar, and certainly don't worry about whether or not I think it's 'good.'" I tell them, "Later, there'll be plenty of time to revise your writing, and finally, to edit it." This was a big shift in thinking for me, because my impression of writing as a kid was that grammar and spelling were what it was all about. I went into teaching with a bit of that same attitude, but I could quickly see how counterproductive it was for the kids. It was like asking them to ride a bike while looking backward.

Everyone knows that kids really respond to the teacher's enthusiasm. But when I first started teaching, I was not only unenthusiastic about teaching writing—I was also pretty scared of it. After a while I could see that my attitudes were rubbing off on the kids, and the classroom atmosphere was in a tailspin. Now I try to get them all motivated about writing before we begin each day by showing them how excited I am about it—not quite like a coach does before a game, but along those lines.

In addition, I like to have a few rituals that we follow. Kids seem to like rituals, and it makes writing time into something special, different from everything else. Writing time begins with my turning off the lights, turning on the desk lamps, and then saying to kids, "On the count of three we're going to leave the school. One, two, three." The music comes on, and they take off. It ends with my saying something like "We have to come back to school now. Three, two, one." I turn on the lights as the kids write down their last thoughts. Years ago my aunt was studying psychology and she told me about hypnosis where they used this counting trick to have people go into hypnosis and then come out of it. Maybe some parents would object to hypnosis, but hey, it really helps their writing.

Every year I try out new techniques for changing the classroom environment, but foremost in my mind is the kids' attitude. If they don't have a good attitude about writing, the atmosphere is always spoiled. I tell my students how important I think writing is, not for me, but for them. "It's the one time in your day when you can truly express yourself, and I look forward to getting to know you through your writing."

Sometimes I tell them about a former student of mine in Japan who was selectively mute. She said nothing in class, and hadn't since she had begun at the school as a kindergartner. She didn't talk, but she had so much to say. It was through her writing that I got to know her. Not only was she a fantastic writer, but she was incredibly talkative and outgoing in her writing.

I like to share this story with my students because it helps them see that writing is not about filling in the correct response, but is, rather, a means of self-expression and communication with others. Once my students understand the value of writing, they come to value the guidelines, rituals, and routines we establish that are necessary for the writing process to work effectively. They don't always buy into it right away, but once they get into their first writing piece, they appreciate what I'm trying to do for them. With that first writing piece in their portfolio, they have all succeeded at writing, and they're part of the club now. Their confidence is growing, and they're willing to take some risks. Writing is no longer a time when some kids get it and most don't; this is a time when everyone, even apathetic Robert, can give it his best shot and really shine on any given day. Once you and your students have developed this writing atmosphere through your classroom environment, you'll be operating on a higher plane, and your students' writing will begin to flourish. The adventure has begun.

Teaching Tips

Lighting: Natural light and incandescent lights are more soothing than fluorescent lights. They make the classroom feel more like a living room, and students will be more comfortable writing here.

Sounds: Eliminate distracting sounds, such as talking, pencil sharpeners, the opening and closing of doors, and the scraping of chairs on hard floors.

Guidelines for Writing Time: Develop a set of guidelines to minimize distracting noises and maintain an atmosphere where imagination can flourish.

Music: Use a variety of music to create different moods. Listen to all sorts of music and select pieces that will enhance the mood required for each writing experience. If you want to use music with singing, select music sung in foreign languages so that the words don't become a distraction.

Teacher's Enthusiasm: Kids will become engaged through your enthusiasm more than anything else. Refer to them as "writers," encourage them to read samples of their writing aloud, congratulate their efforts, highlight their successes, and write along with them when possible.

Rituals: Part of developing an environment for writing is making it different from the rest of school. Establish your own set of writing-time rituals with your students. Try dimming the lights, putting on music, using different writing tools, whatever makes writing time special and unique.

Kids' Attitude: Everything else in writing depends on attitude. Do whatever it takes to get your students excited about writing and feeling that they have something important to say. Work to maintain this throughout the year. Help them see writing as a sacred part of their day.

Chapter 3

Character Development

Although my kids were becoming more descriptive in their writing, they still really struggled with developing characters. And we would need strong characters if we ever hoped to write great adventure stories. The characters in their comic strip stories were often nothing more than hollow stick figures with names (usually named after a friend or a pet). So I decided to distill the process of developing a character into a manageable task. My first attempts were failures; all I got from the kids were physical descriptions—the color of their hair and eyes—but nothing beyond that. It occurred to me that a good character is not defined by physical characteristics but by some intangible essence—their personality, their soul, their eccentricities—and that this is not easy to distill or even comprehend without serious thought.

After several failed attempts, I thought that perhaps if my students didn't see the character but heard the character's voice, they might do a better job of describing him or her. I searched through my music collection to find solo music vocalists who sing with passion. These were great prompts, and the students would certainly be inspired by their music. I tried it first on my own, and it almost worked. Except that I kept being distracted by the words in the music; a particular song may be a story, but not necessarily their story. So I decided to choose music sung in a foreign language that my students would not understand.

In class we had discussed characters. I asked my kids to think of a strong person in their lives. "Now think about how you would describe this person," I asked. They all shared ideas, which I wrote on the board. Predictably, almost all the descriptions contained physical characteristics. I pointed this out and pressed them to come up with other sorts of traits related to personality. "Imagine that you're blind and can't see a new person you meet—how might you describe her?" I made a second list of these responses.

Then it was time to try it out. I turned off the fluorescent overhead lights, turned on the incandescent desk lamps, did my counting backward thing, and played the music. I asked the kids to describe the person who was making the music. "What emotion do you hear in her music? What is this person trying to tell you about herself through her music?" I asked. It was very tough to do, but once they realized that there wasn't a right answer, and once they got over the impulse to describe the musician's physical features, they took off.

It was absolutely incredible to see the variety of characters that emerged from a few songs of a single musician. We took turns reading our writing aloud. The kids were amazed at these differences, and this led to a great discussion about individual interpretation, how each of us perceives the world around us differently and there isn't a right or wrong way of doing this. Each day that week I brought in a different musician who sang in a different foreign language. An amazing variety of characters came out on their papers.

In fact, the unique qualities of each artist really came through in the students' work. At first all we noticed were the differences in the writing, but as the week went on, we started to notice similarities on a broader scale. Some pieces of music were melancholy, and that sadness found its way into the character descriptions. Others were serene, others were joyous, powerful, or mystical in quality. All of this came out in a variety of forms through the student writing.

The following week we went back to our writing. I asked the kids again to think about the strong person they had chosen for our first discussion. I asked them to think about what made those people the way that they are. What shaped their personalities? We had another great discussion about how one's personality is often formed by life events and that these should be included in a character description. Now I asked them to look at their writing samples. "If you think this person is sad, what has made her sad? If she's filled with longing, what is she longing for? If she is overwhelmed with joy, what makes her so happy? What events led up to this moment in time when she is making this music?" I asked. I played each music selection again as they enriched their characters with history, with what actors call backstory when they prepare for a role. Again we shared ideas and students read samples aloud to the class. This always served as a time of celebration and motivation. The kids and I were blown away as the characters came alive, as they deepened and became more complex. There was real emotion, thought, care, creativity, and detail in this writing. Forget about the spelling and mechanics, the substance was beautiful and tangible.

I was amazed by the pictures the students developed in their minds as they listened—a testament to their unencumbered imaginations. Listening to the rhythms and voice of Cuban salsa legend Eliades Ochoa, one of my creative fifth graders, Marion, wrote:

> He strolls through the desert, singing in his loud, deep voice. His long unkempt grey hair and beard blow in the gentle wind. His clothes are torn and patched and ragged, but he does not care.

The music of Dulce Pontes inspired Kathy to create a character full of energy and emotion, both lively and pensive, much like the music itself.

> When she dances, her dress sways and spins. Her brown eyes flash in the light as she dances to the fast music. Her hair is blowing wildly . . .
>   Night time creeps slowly up on the woman's house. Sun light replaced with the light of the stars and the moon. Her white curtains blow in the gentle breeze of the wind. She pulls the covers over her. While she is lying down, she looks to the stars. She dreams about when she was a small child, looking up at the stars with her father. . . . She smiles and falls into a deep sleep, and dreams.

As we read the final drafts aloud we could see how far we had come as a class, as writers. This ability to see characters for more than the superficial, more than as just caricatures, remained a part of their newfound writer's insight. Complexity of character entered their vocabulary for use in future writing.

By this point writers like Heather, the quiet introvert with a natural gift for writing, were soaring. She realized that writing was not a means of doing well in her schoolwork, but a means of communicating and expressing her ideas and emotions. For kids like Robert, who still struggled with grammar, spelling, and organization, writing had become less about school and more about something personal. Writing allowed him to find a bit of himself that he never thought existed.

For some kids, like Robert and a few others, this task was still quite abstract. Even though they had become interested in the process, they weren't able to make it fully work. So I struggled to find ways to make this character-development process more accessible for everyone. As I often do when I get stuck, I called Pete one morning and asked him how he developed characters in his own writing. He gave me some great tools to use in class when he reminded me that characters don't float in space; they're grounded somewhere; they're connected to a place. He talked about how he meets interesting people when he travels and how he sees them as being integrally tied to the land where they live. He pointed to his own investigations into how characters' environments affect them and become a part of them.

He said:

Nothing is more exciting than meeting new and interesting folks. On every trip, a variety of people come into my life—old people, young people, experts, average people. They all have stories. A big part of my job is to capture them and their stories on paper.

This is one of the challenges I love about writing. Beyond physical characteristics, one way to capture a person's mojo, for lack of a better word, is to listen to what they say or watch them do their work or sit with them when they're with their families. Observing what people say and what they do is very important if a writer is to describe them accurately.

So it's the context as much as the physical person that I observe. What do they choose to put on the walls of their houses? How do they interact with others, and with their family? Where do they live and why? What do they eat?

The next thing I look for is what they say and how they say it. Dialogue is a great way to describe someone. Much more important than the freckles on their faces, the tone and syntax of their speech is key to the root of a person. I search for their roots, the depths of character—what makes them tick.

Developing character has to be one of the best parts of my job—meeting and listening to and looking at and observing all kinds of people all over the world in many languages, then

coming back to my cabin on the lake (or the cabin in my heart) and listening to the tapes I've made of these people, reading the observations I've written down in my journals, and looking at the photos of them before I write. What a job! Love it!!

Partly from my conversations with Pete and partly from trial and error in the classroom, I've made some modifications that have proved helpful. As I begin playing the music, for instance, I now ask my students to imagine a scene where this music is being played. I want them to put the sounds into a context. This is often manageable for them because they've had experience describing settings by now. They begin to describe a beach or a meadow or a mountain village, for example. Once a setting for the music is established, I ask the kids to create a character who will enter this scene—almost like you would in a play. This simple change in my approach has been the key to making this activity a success for all of my students, not just the born writers.

As a great example of this important link between setting and character, I love to read aloud the opening of Hemingway's *Islands in the Stream*, in which he depicts a house clinging to the side of an island cliff overlooking the ocean. We can see this setting and imagine it in all of its details before the owner, Thomas Hudson, is invited into the scene. We see, too, that Thomas Hudson's character is inextricably tied to the island and the house and that they are part of who he is.

The house was built on the highest part of the narrow tongue of land between the harbor and the open sea. It had lasted through three hurricanes and it was built solid as a ship. It was shaded by tall coconut palms that were bent by the trade winds and on the ocean side you could walk out of the door and down the bluff across the white sand and into the Gulf Stream. The water of the Stream was usually a dark blue when you looked out at it when there was no wind. But when you walked out into it there was just the great light of the water over that floury white sand and you could see the shadow of any big fish a long time before he could ever come in close to the beach . . .

A man named Thomas Hudson, who was a good painter, lived there in that house and worked there and on the island the greater part of the year. After one has lived in those latitudes long enough the changes of the seasons become as important there as anywhere else and Thomas Hudson, who loved the island, did not want to miss any spring, nor summer, nor any fall or winter.

Sometimes the summers were too hot when the wind dropped in August or when the trade winds sometimes failed in June and July. Hurricanes, too, might come in September and October and even in early November and there could be freak tropical storms any time from June on. But the true hurricane months have fine weather when there are no storms.

Thomas Hudson had studied tropical storms for many years and he could tell from the sky when there was a tropical disturbance long before his barometer showed its presence. He knew how to plot storms and the precautions that should be taken against them. He knew too what it was to live through a hurricane with the other people of the island and the bond that the hurricane made between all people who had been through it. He also knew that hurricanes could be so bad that nothing could live through them. He always thought, though, that if there was ever one that bad he would like to be there for it and go with the house if she went. (Hemingway 2003, 9–10)

This idea of tying character to setting will come up again later on in the school year as the students write adventure narratives that will contain both setting and character richly intertwined. When showing examples through mentor texts, I like to show a variety of material, so that the kids can see how different authors approach the same task in their own ways.

Since Pete and I work closely together, my students know him and know his writing. I show them how Pete introduces Cruger in *The Lost Treasure of Captain Kidd* by placing this eccentric character in a setting that suits him well. The description of character and setting are woven together to form a picture of the scene in the reader's mind. When we imagine Cruger, we imagine the whole scene, with him in it.

I smelled woodsmoke before I saw the man. A little cave set back into rock hid the chair on which he was sitting. Perhaps forty years old, the man had black wild hair, a long black beard, thick eyebrows all tangled up. He wore a coat with rips along the sleeves. He smelled of woodsmoke and fish. Eyeglasses perched on his nose with a string around his neck made him look like a crazy librarian.

When he spoke, his voice was mean and sharp.

"So it's you again, kid. Back already? Brought a friend, eh?"

When the glasses fell to his chest, he was like nobody I'd ever met in a library.

*Killian, fearless, said, "This is my partner, Alex. Tell him what you
told me about the treasure, would you, Mr. Cruger?" . . .*

*Cruger coughed and laughed at the same time, his laugh like the
bark of a sick dog. Right away I didn't trust him.*

*"But, hey, I was young once," he said. His smile was big and fake.
"This is kids' stuff, right, so why run? You come this far, ain't you? You
want to hear about [Captain] Kidd's gold or not?"*

"Sure," said Killian. "Tell Alex what you told me."

*Fishing tackle—line, hooks, floats, and nets—hung from the wall of
the shelter on nails hammered into the rock. Sooty pots and pans were
scattered everywhere. Fish bones littered the packed dirt of the cave
floor. Two big nets were heaped on the ground near the fire.*

*I noticed some topographic maps in one corner of the cave. Four or
five maps were stuck to the wall with black marks on them. Hundreds of
other maps had been stacked neatly in rows on the floor of the cave.*

"Sit down, kids. Or should I say, my little treasure hunters? Ha!"

We sat on old fish bones, brittle as glass. (2000a, 14–15)

With kids, the more eccentric the character the better. Once they understand the idea of developing characters through writing, they really begin to
have fun with it. Creating eccentric characters of their own, completely fic-
tionalized, is a great task for expanding students' imagination and honing
their writing-craft skills. Later in the year, when my students are beginning
their adventure stories, I usually reintroduce the topic of characters and
have them think about the characters they'd like to meet in their narratives.

Again, I use mentor texts to show how other writers introduce characters.
I show them how Dickens introduces us to Ebenezer Scrooge in *A Christmas
Carol*. They connect with it immediately, because they all know the story.

*Oh! but he was a tight-fisted hand at the grind-stone, Scrooge! a squeez-
ing, wrenching, grasping, scraping, clutching, covetous, old sinner!
Hard and sharp as flint, from which no steel had ever struck out gener-
ous fire; secret, and self-contained, and solitary as an oyster. The cold
within him froze his old features, nipped his pointed nose, shriveled his
cheek, stiffened his gait; made his eyes red, his thin lips blue; and spoke
out shrewdly in his grating voice. A frosty rime was on his head, and on
his eyebrows, and his wiry chin. He carried his own low temperature
always about with him; he iced his office in the dogdays; and didn't thaw
it one degree at Christmas.*

External heat and cold had little influence on Scrooge. No warmth could warm, no wintry weather chill him. No wind that blew was bitterer than he, no falling snow was more intent upon its purpose, no pelting rain less open to entreaty. Foul weather didn't know where to have him. The heaviest rain, and snow, and hail, and sleet, could boast of the advantage over him in only one respect. They often "came down" handsomely, and Scrooge never did.

Nobody ever stopped him in the street to say, with gladsome looks, "My dear Scrooge, how are you? when will you come to see me?" No beggars implored him to bestow a trifle, no children asked him what it was o'clock, no man or woman ever once in all his life inquired the way to such and such a place, of Scrooge. Even the blindmen's dogs appeared to know him; and when they saw him coming on, would tug their owners into doorways and up courts; and then would wag their tails as though they said, "no eye at all is better than an evil eye, dark master!"

But what did Scrooge care? It was the very thing he liked. To edge his way along the crowded paths of life, warning all human sympathy to keep its distance; was what the knowing ones call "nuts" to Scrooge. (2004, 3–4)

The craft of character development is complex, and of course there are differences in how characters are developed for fiction and nonfiction, but with focused lessons and opportunities to write, all kids can be successful at this process. The wonderful thing about characters is that they come up in every genre of writing. In class as we're reading novels, we're continually analyzing characters, comparing characters, and looking at the ways in which writers introduce us to their characters. Through this process in reading, kids build a stronger understanding of character development, which later comes out in their own writing.

Early in the year I work deliberately and specifically on character-development skills through music-writing activities. The kids then take these skills and apply them throughout the entire year. Each time they develop a character in their writing, they understand the process better and improve their skills. Whether it's through poetry, through personal narrative, or through adventure writing, the kids learn how to develop characters and how to incorporate them into their writing, thereby enriching and bringing life to their prose.

Here are two examples of character essays based on the music-writing experiences we had in class. In each one we get a real glimpse into an imaginary character's life. By empathizing with the character, the students are able to attribute emotions and memories in a realistic way.

I was struck by the power of this first essay by Madilyn. Through its simplicity and the weaving of memories, she develops an intriguing character full of longing in just three short paragraphs. She has a graceful style of writing and seems to say just what needs to be said and nothing more.

Young Once More
by Madilyn

(Based on the music of Dulce Pontes)

A woman is singing as she walks through a little town, listening contentedly to the passing sounds of the street. She takes a breath of fresh air and waves kindly to the people walking by. Long, straight, black hair hangs down past her waist. A flower is nestled behind her ear and brings out the color of her eyes. Her elegant dress flows behind her in the breeze. A sad expression forms on her face as she continues to sing. She remembers when she ran around town playing with the dogs on the streets, but she can't do that anymore, for she is too old.

It's amazing how her voice is so strong. Her eyes follow the wheels of a wagon as they roll around, and around. She looks at the horse pulling it, trudging along, its hooves thumping on the hard ground. Her mind drifts off, remembering riding her horse, how the wind felt rushing through her tangled hair.

No longer in the town, she walks through sand. It feels hot on her feet as she slips off her sandals and lies down in the powdery sand. When she was young she loved falling asleep on the beach, listening to the crashing waves as a lullaby. She falls asleep once again, thinking of her past, as the sun's rays beat down on her tan face. She feels young again, lying there in her past once more.

Matt, a quiet and thoughtful kid who loves music, tuned into the melancholy nature of Ochoa's voice and imagined the life of this man as he reminisced about his childhood.

Memories
by Matt

(Based on the music of Eliades Ochoa)

I see a man singing on a beach. The man has light grey hair and looks about fifty years old. He seems happy. He is sitting on a chair with a light brown guitar. A smile is spread across his face. He is happy because he loves to sing and he loves the sound of the music.

He is very joyful today when he sings. He loves the light green palm trees, the tropical flowers, the ocean, and the soft light sheet of sand that covers his feet. That is what he always sings about.

It is early in the morning and the sun is just coming up. The golden sunlight reflects off of the clear, calm water. He is having fun singing. Some others sing and play instruments behind him. There are many string players.

There are palm trees and exotic plants and animals surrounding him. It is a miniature rainforest around him. The sun is almost fully up now and a crowd gathers around to hear him sing. The ocean water, which is now light blue from the sun, washes up onto the shoreline. It is beautiful there. The crowd grows larger as morning leaves.

As more and more people start to watch him, it reminds him of when he was a child. There were men that used to sing there while he watched. He would go there every day to hear them sing. As he watched, he learned how to sing. He used to love to dance to the men's music. They would play late into the night, and they would start again very early in the morning. They always beat the sun. He once woke up at three o'clock in the morning, and snuck out of the house to see if the men were there. He heard them in the distance, but he wanted to make sure. They were already playing by the time that he got there. They would be there every day, now he is there every day. He is now one of them.

The people watching him start to dance, so do the instrument players. He keeps on singing but also starts to dance. His voice is overjoyed like it always is when he remembers. Now he puts his memories away and keeps on singing and dancing in the golden sand.

Teaching Tips

Music: Try out different types of music and different artists for helping students approach the subject of character. I found a few that have worked well for inspiring this sort of writing in my students. I love some of the melancholy yet powerful and graceful songs of Dulce Pontes of Portugal (*Lagrimas, O Primeiro Canto*). Cesaria Evora of Cape Verde also has a melancholy sound in much of her music, but there's also a casually festive mood that emerges in some of her music. Oumou Sangare of Mali (*Worotan*) has a powerful voice embraced by rhythmic and emotionally charged background music. Ibrahim Ferrer (*Buena Vista Social Club*) and Eliades Ochoa (*Sublime Ilusión*) are masters of Cuban salsa. Their voices are powerful, unique, and very expressive of their passion. Grey Ghost is another one of my favorites. He recorded his first CD (and probably his only) at the age of ninety. He sings in English, but his words are difficult to understand, so they don't conflict with the writing. He's an amazing pianist of honky-tonk and swing from an era long gone. His soulful music shows the richness and interest of his character. Cheikh Lo of Senegal blends musical sounds of his native country with sounds of Cuban guajira, reggae, soul, and Brazilian rhythms. I just got his newest CD, *Lamp Fall*, and I can't wait to try it out with my students. Experiment and have fun with it.

Combine Setting and Character: Have students begin by describing a detailed setting (beach, meadow, village, etc.). Then have them create a character who enters this setting. Combining setting and character allows students to create a realistic scene in which the character can become fully developed, and it often makes it easier for students to begin.

Read Mentor Texts: Use a variety of mentor texts to show how different authors combine setting and character, and how they develop characters in different ways. Look for short excerpts from familiar novels to illustrate your point. Read the excerpts aloud, but also give your students a hard copy so that they can refer to it again later.

Sounds: Eliminate distracting sounds like talking, pencil sharpeners, the opening and closing of doors, and the scraping of chairs on hard floors so that your students can focus on the music.

Rituals: Part of developing an environment for writing is making it different from the rest of school. Use your own set of writing time rituals with your students. Try dimming the lights as the music comes on. It has a dramatic effect on student writing.

Step Two

First Steps Toward the Adventure Essay

Chapter 4

Elements of Adventures

I was thrilled that my students were now able to depict settings and develop characters, but when I had them write adventure stories, the results were still disastrous. They were full of detail, but they were just longer now and still quite boring. I tried to dissect their stories to figure out what exactly was missing. I looked at exciting adventure stories by published authors and tried to determine how these differed in a general sense from the stories of my students. One of the biggest things that jumped out at me was the feeling you get, when you're reading a great adventure, that the narrator has never been in this place or this situation before. This is new ground, and it's dangerous, or inspiring, or amazing, but it's definitely a new experience. This is what keeps the reader on the edge of his or her seat. My students tended to write about familiar places and familiar events and try to make them seem daring and adventurous. This just never worked. Sometimes they tried to include imaginary places and situations, but, being young, they didn't have enough knowledge about such places. The results often bordered on the ridiculous because they were too fanciful and highly unrealistic.

One morning over coffee I talked to Pete about my frustration that the kids were so close but still not there. Pete said, "You know, Dave, what they're missing is passion. They're not connecting with the subject of their adventure, and that's what's missing in their writing." He went on to tell me about some of his own struggles with this issue as a writer.

I have a wonderful editor who, when he read my *Mississippi River*, called me to say, "Well, Pete, something's not working. I don't know exactly what it is either." These are not words any writer likes to hear. But I know Larry. I've worked with him for twenty years and when he says something is not working, well, I listen carefully.

Like an effective director in the theater who doesn't *tell* his actors how to act a part, but is more of a catalyst for the actor to discover his or her own role and how to approach the part, Larry continued on the phone, "Something's missing, Pete. Something your Rio Grande book had." Meanwhile I'm thinking, what could that be?

Larry continued, "Some emotional commitment, a personal involvement of some kind. I'm just not getting it in this new book."

Again, Larry was thinking on his feet (or on the phone), and I was trying to think, too—on the phone—but couldn't.

I hung up, frustrated but determined to figure out what I needed to bring this project to life. What emotional truth was I missing? Larry was basically saying the book was flat. This nonfiction adventure book contained all the attendant and necessary parts: it had characters, it had history, it had setting, and it had structure. And it was a true adventure. So what did it need?

I decided I had to journal. So I pulled out a notebook and wrote down all my thoughts about my canoe trip down the Mississippi, and as I was writing, I think it was on the third day, I discovered the problem. I had forgotten to mention and weave through the book the very essence of my journey: my feelings of *fear*. That's what I experienced going down the great, historic, quintessential American river—*fear*. And I hadn't even mentioned that anywhere in the seven-thousand-word book!

Yet all along, first in my research before I took my journey, then during the adventure itself, and even afterward when I was putting it all together, the overriding emotional theme for me was the intimidating vastness of this great mythical river. I didn't just fear the river itself. I wasn't afraid of all that water; I'm an experienced and comfortable paddler. Yes, there were times when I was intimidated by the river's power, especially down at the delta, and in a hurricane no less. But more important, perhaps I was terrified of the subject itself, a massive, unwieldy topic—the Father of all American Rivers. How could anyone, I'd worried, capture this legendary river, this river of American Dreams? And especially in a twenty-page, double-spaced, typewritten manuscript with fifty photos?

No matter how hard it might be, I now knew I needed somehow to layer in the emotional core of fear to my book. As I revised the writing in the next few months, I addressed these issues head-on and gave the book what it needed, its emotional glue. And I think it's a better book because of this.

At the core of every essay, every journey, every book about a journey, every adventure, is passion, feeling. Passion can take many forms—love, hate, and fear are the most obvious—and it is crucially important that a writer record his passion about places and people and ideas. Not that you're always going to talk about these feelings directly, but they will inevitably come out in the writing. Every good piece of writing has a point of view—in some ways, it's all subjective—and this attitude of the writer gives the paragraphs their strength and energy. Nonfiction does not live in a vacuum where all sides are presented equally. Nonfiction is not merely accurate reporting.

Whenever I travel I am enthralled and excited, but I'm also scared, bored, fearful, depressed, terrified, and sometimes happy beyond belief. Snakes, like the fer-de-lance, cross my trail in the Mexican jungle. Powerful whirlpools nearly sink my canoe in the upper Missouri River. And I react with all kinds of fears on top of other passions. There is truth to the adages "no pain, no gain" and "nothing ventured, nothing gained." Something like, suffering leads to knowledge.

So, Dave, if the kids in your class don't have anything at stake, if they're not passionate about their subject, how can they write anything worthwhile? How can they enter into the details of a story without feeling invested? They don't even have to use the first-person pronoun. I just wrote a book about an Arctic whale scientist and never once said "I." There's not even an author photo in the author bio on the flap of the book. Yet the passion I felt for Craig George's work with the Iñupiaq Eskimos of Alaska as he collected samples of whales during

their whale harvests is on every page. My love for the subject, I think, infuses the whole book.

Adventure and writing adventure stories really demand personal involvement. How are you going to get that from the kids in your classroom? That's up to you, Dave.

Later that day I looked at a couple of Pete's books to see how his connection to the setting and his passion for the adventure itself come out in his writing. This was what I was looking for. I looked at *Lost Treasure of the Inca*:

The treasure could not be hidden in a better location to foil treasure hunters. The craggy Llanganati Mountains are rugged beyond belief. Cloaked in bewitching fog, they are nearly impassable. To this day the Llanganatis are called "the mountains of electricity and earthquakes" because of the numerous electrical storms and constant earth tremors there. Parts have never been mapped. Aerial photographs often reveal nothing but a vast blanket of cloud.

Most treasure hunters believe the gold was hidden on a fifteen-thousand-foot volcano in the Llanganatis called Cerro Hermoso, or Beautiful Mountain. To reach the volcano I would have to hike for three days. They said I would encounter snow, rain, sleet, fog, and even earthquakes. The trek would take me through a cloud forest of gnarled jungle so thick it might take days to move only a few miles. Around fourteen thousand feet, I would begin to slog through the high Andean plateau country called páramo. The páramo of the Llanganatis is littered with quaking bogs—huge clumps of soggy earth floating in muck, a quicksand of marsh and mud . . .

After what seemed like endless hours of hard climbing, suddenly we were out of the dense jungle. The sky opened above us like a gray wound, and now we sat on the tabletop of the world. This was the páramo.

The páramo at 14,000 feet is a boggy, barren, wet, slushy desert. It has its own traps in store for treasure hunters, such as cacti and thorns, but at least now we could see for long distances. We were no longer boxed in by the cloud-covered jungle.

In fact, the sky seemed to swoop down on us. The fog was alive. Unlike the fog anywhere in the world, the Llanganati fog moves not in one direction, but in all directions at the same time. For hours it drizzled and sleeted and even hailed a few times as the fog darted madly around the hills and the lakes. . . . (2002, 9, 32)

Now I knew what I needed. I needed to take my kids to unfamiliar places where they could explore something completely new to them. Where their emotions would be fresh. Only in this way would the narrator's feelings about the setting of the adventure carry through to the reader. We were ready to depart from the backyard adventures in search of the lost silver dollar and head out into undiscovered territory. To do this I wanted to get them out of the school, at least in their minds, and into a completely new, fresh place. If the writer wasn't experiencing a sense of wonderment as he wrote, then the reader certainly couldn't be expected to experience it either.

My first experiment was simply to project a slide from my own travels while playing some background music. I tried a few different settings; one was a jungle clearing in the Brazilian rain forest. One was a snowy trail leading up along a steep cliff into the clouds in the Sangre de Cristo Mountains of New Mexico. Another one was a view out across a rocky barren cliff, down to a desert valley below with the Anasazi ruins of Chaco Canyon visible up against the cliff base. Each image was clearly a faraway, magical place that invited exploration.

To add to the scene I wanted music, but music that would enhance rather than detract from the original goal. For the Brazilian jungle scene I chose a few tracks from the soundtrack to the movie *The Mission*. The powerful, elegant, haunting music, rich with woodwinds and native flutes, created a mysterious and somewhat daunting feeling. I wanted them to imagine the feeling of traveling into uncharted jungle.

I paired the snowy mountain trail with selections from the Gregorian chants. Here I played around with time setting too, as the harmonious chants brought to mind the endless journeys of monks traveling through the Alps hundreds of years ago.

The Chaco Canyon desert scene was paired with excerpts from Peter Gabriel's *Passion*. This instrumental collage of percussion and Arabic instruments and sounds brought images of the Sahara and galloping horses to mind for me. I intentionally did not tell the kids where any of these scenes were located, nor did I give them information about the music, so as not to give them my preconceived notions or have them bring up any of their own. Before we began each writing session, I simply stated that we were about to embark on an adventure. I would follow this by saying that on the count of three we were going to leave the school and go to another world. Then I would turn out the lights, count slowly to three, turn on the slide, and start the music. I asked the kids to try to include three things in their writing. "Describe the scene, tell what you've come here to explore, and express your thoughts and emotions about being in this strange new land."

I found that this synthesis of music and scene was amazingly motivating to kids. Every kid would write and write and wouldn't want to stop. They would really be lost in these other worlds for a time. The sensory input in an otherwise dark space seemed to focus their attention and bombard them with strong impulses to leave the school and go to these other worlds in their minds. I made each writing session progressively longer so that the final one lasted for nearly an hour. In spite of this, most of the kids were still writing furiously to get down their last thoughts as we "returned to school" at the countdown from three to one.

We took time to read our writing aloud. It amazed me that even with the same multisensory prompt, students still had incredibly varied experiences—each completely fresh in a new and unfamiliar scene. A feeling of awe was now present in their writing—the sense that the narrator was experiencing this place for the first time. The level of interest and suspense was instantly magnified in their writing, and they could all see it.

From here the next logical step was video. I was looking for something that would provide multiple scenes, evoke a mood, and imply some action, which would be necessary for an adventure to take place. I wrestled with the challenge of creating a video that had specific images corresponding to selected music. Eventually I figured out a way to create my own movies using music and downloaded video clips. The process was time-consuming, but incredibly worthwhile.

When coming up with an idea for a new movie, I like to start with the music. Instrumental soundtracks are a great choice because they don't have words to distract the kids, but they're often composed to accompany a scene. I select a piece of music and listen to it over and over, trying to imagine the scene that seems perfect for the music. Then I jot down any words associated with the scene that might serve as keywords in a search. For example, I imagine a desolate scene with blowing snow, so I might write, "tundra, Siberia, North Pole, blizzard, ice cap." Using an educational video search engine, I type in these keywords and see what comes up. I watch the video clips, splice sections together, and synchronize the whole thing with the music. The movie doesn't have to be particularly high quality, and it doesn't need to be more than a few minutes long. I usually make it so that the music and video begin at the same time, but after a few minutes the video fades to black and the music continues playing. This provides the students with some powerful images in a short amount of time, and they can keep writing with only the music, making new visuals in their mind's eye.

Since we can't take the students to the tundra, maybe we can bring the tundra to the students. These little movies serve as a means of doing exactly that—bringing the world into the classroom. And it's into the world that they will be taking their adventures.

A simpler alternative to this video-making process is to combine still images with music using a program like Microsoft's Photo Story 3 or Soundslides. These programs allow you, simply and quickly, to import photos and music and combine them to create a "movie" of your own. Using the "Ken Burns effect" feature, the still images pan and zoom to create the illusion of movement, which is very effective. This process is so easy to use that you can create an incredibly powerful multimedia writing prompt in no time at all. I'm no technological wizard, so this is really very easy to do (see the "Teaching Tips" at the end of this chapter for more details). I also talk about the specific steps in making these movies in Chapter 8.

No matter how you create these multimedia writing prompts, you can easily integrate other areas of the curriculum as well. If you're a sixth-grade teacher, for example, your students might be learning about ancient world cultures. You could select photos or video clips of archaeological landmarks of Egypt, Greece, or Rome and use this writing activity in combination with your students' research as a means of enriching your social studies instruction. If you're a third-grade teacher focusing on rain-forest ecosystems in your science class, you could select images and videos of rain forests to create a writing prompt that will engage your students in writing with your science content as a backdrop. You can couple the images with music of the Amazonian rain forest to enhance the effect. So how you create these writing prompts will depend on what you're teaching and how you want to engage your students, but there's no limit to the number of possibilities.

By setting up a variety of these video lessons, I can focus on different aspects of adventure writing and build in lessons on plot development. Each session is not a full story, but rather a small vignette, where you can hone specific writing elements while keeping the students completely engaged in the material. Eventually all the lessons learned here will be brought together in the larger and more complete adventure writing project. The subject of the lessons really depends on the writing needs of the kids; each year the needs are slightly different, and I modify the lessons accordingly.

I design these movies with the teaching of a specific element of writing in mind. In other words, I think about an aspect that I want to address in my students' writing, and then I design a video which will bring out that aspect of their writing and allow them to work on it. At the start of each writing lesson I give them a few ideas to focus on and pair the areas of focus with the appropriate video clip.

For example, I might say, "In today's adventure I want you to focus on building suspense. Don't let the reader know too much too soon. Keep them guessing, wondering, anticipating." The video for this lesson will unfold slowly, each step revealing a bit more of an awe-inspiring scene, giving hints at what might be to come. The music that accompanies the video is a bit ominous, the tension mounting gradually with mysterious background instruments.

During another lesson I ask the kids to try to let the reader know that the scene takes place in the distant past without telling the reader explicitly. I might do this because I've seen a need for more subtlety in their descriptions. So I say something like, "You don't want to hit the reader over the head with the setting by telling them what it is; instead you want them to experience it for themselves. You can do this best by showing them the scene and letting them come to conclusions on their own (showing as opposed to telling)." For this video, I choose images and video clips that depict the Middle Ages, coupled with the music of Loreena McKennitt, which is inspired by ancient Celtic songs. I tell the kids, "Show me in your writing, through your descriptions, that the scene is from long ago and far away." And they inevitably rise to the challenge.

One year, Kris, who got right into the scene and created vivid images, began with, "Twang, my bowstring sings when the arrow takes flight . . ." He followed this up with crisp details of a furious battle.

> Galloping faster, I charge toward the castle blowing my horn, the bells toll out and the gates open . . . "Quickly shut the gates, all men to the Ramparts, archers ready." I say pausing to catch my breath, "The Swampers are coming." . . . the archers let fly a volley of arrows that slice through their front lines . . . The Swampers return with bellowing cries and crude projectiles flung with enough force to shatter bone, but not armor or the brick of our castle.

Before watching a movie about ancient Maya ruins, I tell the kids, "Use your words to show the reader that this is new and uncharted ground. Show the reader through your descriptions that you've never seen anything like this before; maybe no one has ever seen this before. Give the reader a sense of awe and discovery without saying it directly." I usually follow this up with a few examples or by reading a small snippet from an adventure story.

Then I dim the lights, roll the movie, and watch the kids as they imagine themselves in the incredible scenes (when possible, I like to use a multimedia projector and a large screen, so that the effects are more dramatic). I tell them that the end of the video is their invitation to begin writing. As the screen goes black and the music continues, they dive into this other world and create amazing stories, rich with detail. At this point in the year, they're used to writing with detail, so their descriptions no longer come across as hollow, and elements of plot are becoming evident.

These activities have proved to me that all kids have amazing imaginations; it's just a matter of tapping into them. Even the most reluctant writer will write volumes when thrown into the middle of an adventure and asked to write his way out. A few years ago one of my passionate fifth-grade writers, Gabriella, looked frustrated at the end of one of these adventure vignettes. When I asked her if she was all right, she said, "I'm just mad because my hand can't keep up with my mind." That's what I was shooting for—an adventure (even an imaginary adventure) so true to life that it draws the writer in completely.

With the skills developed during these writing sessions, the kids are now ready to take on the task of developing their adventure projects. These will be detailed narratives, rich in descriptive language, full of voice, crafted with structural elements in place, and supported by the students' research.

Following is an example of an essay that Marion created as she imagined what it would be like to come upon the ruins of an ancient city. In these few short paragraphs, she accurately conveys the sense that she is in new and uncharted territory, and the reader can experience this discovery right along with her.

The Ancient City
by Marion

(Based on a slide of Chaco Canyon with Peter Gabriel's *Passion* playing in the background)

I come over the hill, walking barefoot on the hot, hard clay ground. Below me is an ancient city, walls once huge, now crumbling around it, all made of . . . what is that? Clay? Brick? Wood? Stone? It's hard to tell from up here . . . A once flowing riverbed now lies dried and dead in the background. A jackrabbit hops down one of the long deserted paths, a bramble clump rolls through another. I must look at it up close.

I make my way down the hill into this incredibly old place. I stumble, and slide down a few feet before I regain my balance. I am now in the village and I see one solitary log sticking out of the wall. How did that get there? There are no trees around here . . . There are many buildings here, some up to five stories high! They look to be made out of neatly packed stones held together and covered with adobe. They are so old, how old? I wish to know. The roofs of the buildings are caving in, not nearly as grand as in their glory I'm sure, worn away by years and years of wind and the yearly downpour of rain, quickly scorched away by the ever-burning sun.

Light is beginning to fade now, and I begin my ascent up the hill and back to my camp. As I walk I am mentally sketching an image of the city in its glory years. That image will reign in my dreams tonight.

Teaching Tips

Making Video Writing Prompts

Music: I always begin by selecting a piece of music that evokes strong images, such as Peter Gabriel's *Passion* or the haunting melodies of Loreena McKennitt. Often soundtracks work well, especially ones without words, because they're frequently designed to accompany images. Some of my favorites are from: *Havana, The Mission, Gladiator, Lord of the Rings, Motorcycle Diaries, Frida, Himalaya*, and *Memoirs of a Geisha*. Find music that appeals to you, and you'll be more successful in making videos with it.

Video Clip Source: I use Discovery Education videos (http://streaming.discoveryeducation.com). If your school does not subscribe to this service, they have a free thirty-day trial membership. This database of educational videos covers an endless array of possible topics. There are probably many other similar databases available in your area.

Selecting Video Clips: Listen to the music you've selected and jot down keywords that come to mind. Use these keywords in your search for video clips within Discovery Education or a similar database.

Microsoft Movie Maker: I've used Movie Maker (often comes standard with PCs) to create video prompts. Create a new video using this program. Insert your downloaded video clips into your new video track (note: you can also insert still images). Next, insert your music tracks into the soundtrack of your video. Now edit your video clips until you have the video that you want. Adjust it to align with your music selections. Set the audio narration that comes with the educational videos to mute, so that you hear only your music. Click through the finishing touches, and you're ready to go. I've heard that Pinnacle and iMovie are also excellent programs for creating similar videos. Another option is to use videos recorded from your own camera if you'd like.

Photo Story 3: This program is a free download. It enables you to combine still photos and music in a remarkable way that makes them into a presentation that feels like a video. With a few easy steps you download photos, either from your own files or from a website. You can arrange them and rearrange them in any order you choose. You can even add in a layer of text if you'd like (on the opening slide as a title, for example). There are also options to change the transitions, the time that each photo is visible, and many other details about the photos. Then you import music from saved files. When you're finished making the desired adjustments, the program mixes the media to create a video that pans and zooms through your selected photos as music plays in the background. Soundslides is also an excellent program, but I don't think it's a free download. In searching for photos, you can use your own images, or you can search online. TrekEarth has an amazing array of beautiful photos from all over the world—just use the search tool within this website to locate the photos you want (http://www.trekearth.com/gallery).

Chapter 5

Adventure Writing

Soon the kids were getting the hang of adventure writing. Through their reading and through their video adventure writing experiences, it was all starting to come together. Their stories now included the elements of adventure in a fresh and captivating way, and reading them was a pleasure. The kids could see it too, and they were energized by it.

It was about this time in the evolution of my trial-and-error writing program that I saw an opportunity to do something far more challenging and far more rewarding. The stories that my kids were writing were wonderful, but I wasn't sure they went far enough. They lacked a deeper sense of understanding about the setting. Their descriptions were based solely on their observations of the videos I had created, and in that sense they were totally authentic. But apart from their observations, the kids had no real knowledge of the subject. Maybe, I thought, they could conduct research online, and then infuse it with their imaginative storytelling to create an even better, more authentic, more grounded essay. I could ask them to travel to places in their imaginations based on what they discovered about a place on the Internet. And what would it be then, would it be fiction or nonfiction? Or could it be both? I wasn't sure.

In another helpful conversation with Pete, I asked how he was able so seamlessly to blend his passionate storytelling with his research. I wanted to learn about his process so that I could attempt to use it as a model to pull fiction and nonfiction together in my own classroom. Some aspects would clearly have to be different (my kids didn't actually go to places as Pete does), but maybe the concept and the process could be the same. If this were possible, I thought, it would not only breathe new life into my social studies research projects, but it would also add something important to the kids' adventure writing.

I knew Pete would have some interesting ideas on the subject because a nonfiction writer applies artifice in order to tell a true story. He has limited space and time, so knowing how to begin and end a story is crucial. Setting, of course, is key, as are pacing and character development. There's also an arc to any piece of writing, be it fiction or nonfiction.

Pete and I had many long discussions about this. He explains it best:

Adventure Writing: The Craft of Weaving Fiction and Nonfiction

Fiction, in part, draws its creative power from reality, from real people in real places, in real history. Nonfiction draws its power from the same places, people, and facts. How a writer uses information to support either a nonfiction or a fiction piece is an essential aspect of the craft of writing. Call it artifice.

My two novelist friends Jean Craighead George and Will Hobbs are perfect examples of writers who love to write fiction because they like to travel to interesting places to do their research. They are explorers. Before they write, while they write, and often after they write, they travel to places where they explore their subjects, meet people, interview scientists in the same manner that we nonfiction writers interview scientists and talk to experts. They smell the air and listen to the sounds of places. That's the nature of research. Research is the exploration of a subject. If Will Hobbs is writing a novel about the Anasazi of the Southwest, he goes there to smell the place, walk its ruins, talk to the park rangers, and so much more. Jean George journeyed to the Arctic many times when she was writing _Julie of the Wolves_. She still goes back to visit her son, Craig, an Arctic whale biologist. New books have come from repeated visits.

Writers explore their subjects in the real world. The idea that fiction exists somewhere outside reality is a myth. While setting up for a school presentation in an elementary school library last year, I heard a well-intentioned, overworked librarian say to a large class of first graders, "Now kids, what does the *f* stand for in *fiction*?" Silence. "You know, you do." Fidgety silence. "Class, you know it stands for *fake*. Fiction is fake and nonfiction is not fake, nonfiction is true."

Fiction, truth to be told, is based on information and research as much as nonfiction is. And there are people who argue that fiction is even truer than nonfiction simply because it accurately captures what is deeply real within the human condition. But that's another conversation for another time.

Putting it all together isn't so easy. One key aspect of the craft of writing is learning how to take one's research (information/facts/history) and weave it into one's text, essay, story, or what have you.

Some writers can do this more smoothly than others. I'm not sure there is a list of techniques that I could share with student writers. Much of this seamless bonding of information into one's text is learned from reading writers who do it well. And of course from endless practice. Practice practice practice. Read read read.

"So what is your process?" I wanted to know. "How do you make this work? Take me through it step by step, so that I can try to replicate this with my students within my own classroom," I said. And here's what Pete came up with:

The Adventure Writing Process

Whether the final result of my work is a story, an article, or a book, the writing process involves three stages. First, I engage my imagination in the adventure before me—with growing anticipation I focus on preparation and research. Next, there's the excitement and unfolding adventure of the journey itself. Finally, I settle down to the last part of the creative process by drawing together the threads of my research and experience into a story that can touch the lives of my readers.

Preparation and Research

As I tell students in my writing workshops, research is one of the most fun things I do as a nonfiction writer and as a traveler. Before a trip, during a trip, and after a trip, I conduct research. Other words for research include *study, discover, explore*, and *investigate*.

A lot of people think research is something dry and dusty that happens in old libraries. It's true that some research does indeed take place in old—and new—libraries. Articles and books are very important in preparing for a river trip, for instance. They can give me a mental picture of the experience ahead, which can be important in planning what I should bring and making special arrangements, ranging from the need for a passport to warm clothes. Articles and books can also give me ideas of things to look for in my adventure. Learning about experiences writers have had in the past can clue me in to important aspects of the river that may have changed. Is wildlife as plentiful as it once was? Are people using the river as they did in past times? Are there now dams where there once were wild, flowing waters and deep canyons? I certainly read before I go. I also read during a trip, and afterward. Books are a great resource. But there are other ways to research a river.

People, for instance. Every river has its experts. Not only scientists and ecologists and historians, but just plain people like dads and moms, or the man and woman down the street, or especially grandparents. Older people have a lot of wisdom stored inside them and love to talk about what they know, including river stories, river events, and river lore. Most of us are better talkers than listeners. I often ask writing students to listen to their grandparents, and collect stories and information and expertise that might later go into a piece of writing.

The first thing I do when I'm about to take a trip on a river is start a list of articles and books to read and people to talk to. Whether it's a trip on the Hudson, the Mississippi, the Missouri, the Amazon, the Everglades, the Yukon, the Rio Grande, or Otter Creek outside my window, I need to find out who the experts are. I can talk to them in person, or I can talk to them on the phone. Or I can write them a letter or an e-mail.

Other methods of research in preparing for a river trip include fun things like learning what gear to take. On the Hudson River, I needed a long canoe for long distances and big water. On the Erie Canal I needed a shorter, faster, slightly tippier canoe. This was something I discovered as I began to learn about the waterway I'd chosen to travel and to write about. At the same time I was learning about boats, in preparation for my Mississippi trip, I checked the Internet and found all kinds of information. I also found two people who had canoed the entire river, and I contacted them via e-mail. When we spoke on the phone, they gave me excellent advice, and even hooked me up with one of the Mississippi paddlers in New Orleans. He helped me with some photography, and gave me some river facts I did not know before.

The Journey

Once I've prepared as best I can for a river trip; once I've read some articles and books and websites about the river; and once I've talked to as many river experts as I can locate, I am now more familiar with the watershed I'll be traveling. After I plan the trip as best I can, making an itinerary of where I hope to be on any given day, (even though some of these plans fall through, other opportunities appear out of nowhere), I am ready to embark. I have an outline, one I can change as events occur, as I move down the river.

I often call the journey itself research. An adventure down a river is learning, exploring, investigating, isn't it? I take river books with me so I can learn details along the way. I talk to experts on the river banks. I stop in towns I didn't even know existed. Most important, though, I observe the river firsthand. No research is as good as firsthand observation. I smell the river, I see it, I hear it, and I feel it in the rocking of the canoe in the waves. All of which—impressions, history, facts, interviews—I write down in my journal.

Journals

Journals are a way of recording one's firsthand research. The river journal I keep will form the basis of the book I will write when I get home. I have kept up to a thousand pages of journal notes for a twenty-page children's manuscript and a three-hundred-page adult book.

My research while I'm on the expedition is intense. From the moment I wake at four or five in the morning to the moment I fall asleep after a long day of hard travel, I keep my eyes and ears open. I value curiosity, and I ask a ton of questions. Anything I learn that I think might be useful later, I write down in my journal. Or, more accurately, I speak into a microphone and then transcribe when I get home, for these days I make my notes with a tape recorder. Notebooks, I discovered, get awfully wet in the rain and the spray of whitewater. I have returned from river trips with notebooks I can't read. So a few years ago I started to use a micro-cassette recorder, which I store in a waterproof pouch around my neck. (Buying just the right pouch is part of my preparation for a journey.) I also bring an inexpensive point-and-shoot camera to take snapshots that later will help me with visual detail.

The Writing

After completing my journey down a river, it's time to write the book. The hardest thing for me is to hammer out a first draft. And why shouldn't it be difficult? A blank page sits before me, and now I have to make something from nothing.

To make the task less daunting, I take one step at a time. Just like climbing a mountain. I don't focus on the summit, the finished product, but on smaller tasks. On the little steps before me. The first thing I do is type out all the notes I've taken on my tape recorder. Usually that's about ninety pages of text. Sometimes it's a lot more; other times it's less.

After the notes are typed, I go to a quiet place. I need utter concentration when I work on an essay, a story, or a book. Often this is in my cabin. Four or five in the morning is my most productive time, but I work through the day with intermittent walks.

On my first morning of work, I review my notes, leaf through history books about the river at hand, then put everything aside. I try to think how best to tell the story of my adventure. I want the adventure to come alive. I want the reader to feel the adventure the way I felt it. So I think about structure, about beginning, middle, and end. I think about pace, the speed of the story. I think about tone, how the words sound. And I recall my feelings as I went down the river. What was I passionate about, what made me most afraid or excited?

I work for many hours, but end up with about three pages a day, some days fewer, some days more. I try not to edit myself too much the first time around. I want to get at the heart of an adventure, its feeling. Thinking too much about my writing can stop me dead in my tracks. So I tend to overwrite and come up with too many pages, much of which I'll have to cut out later.

After five or six days, I complete a rough draft of a short book. It's usually very rough—pretty bad, actually—and ten to fifteen pages too long. But I let it sit for a day, then rewrite it before sending it to my editor. I know it still needs a lot of work.

When published, the book will be forty-eight pages. That means I have to come up with a twenty-page manuscript, typed and double-spaced, about six to seven thousand words. I also send about three hundred photographs from my journey. These are often taken with my new digital single-lens reflex camera. No more than fifty of these will end up in the book.

After I send the book off, I wait for my editor's call. Sometimes he doesn't call for weeks. This is hard. When he calls, we talk about the draft. This begins the editing process. When he says it needs work, I admit I feel disappointed, but I know he's right. He sees things I can't see because I'm too close to the material. He helps me with the overall thinking of the story. He asks me questions like: Should this be in the present tense? Can I add some history here? Can I shorten this passage? How might I tighten the prose in places? Or bigger questions like, don't you think some emotional core to the story is missing? Ugh.

Always his comments are helpful. There are, of course, times that I don't agree with him. For six months we edit. We edit by talking over the phone, we edit by fax, and we edit on computer disks and e-mail attachments. I rewrite again and again. Gradually the book takes shape.

Understanding Pete's process allowed me to begin looking for ways to implement this in my own classroom. I found that our two worlds of writing, that of the journalist and the teacher, shared some common elements. I also found ways to use the tools of technology to substitute for elements that at first seemed impossible to re-create in the classroom; and I found that other elements would just need some alterations. Preparation and planning could happen in much the same way, by thinking through the journey, finding materials that would be needed later on like maps and Web sites, and planning ahead through research. The journey itself would have to be quite different from taking an actual adventure, and this is where a substitution was necessary. In order for students to take their journey, we would use the Internet to explore every step of the way. We would combine notes from multiple Web sites as Pete uses field notes. And we could use images and perhaps video clips with other interactive media like Google maps to create this virtual journey. Our writing process would now take place in a similar fashion to Pete's process—a compilation of research and field notes could be woven around a narrative thread and, with any luck, we would seamlessly blend fiction and nonfiction.

Step Three

The Adventure Writing Project

Chapter 6

Research

Each year I have my kids choose a state to research and write an essay about. The project incorporates many aspects of the curriculum, including history and geography. It was the perfect venue to try out my adventure writing ideas.

My friend and teaching partner, Brett Adams, and I talked at length about how to make Pete's adventure writing process work in the classroom. Brett is a special education teacher, so he was looking at this project from a slightly different angle. His advice was to break the project into manageable chunks to avoid overwhelming the kids. Together, we created an outline of the process, breaking it into manageable sections. We later found that we needed to break it down even more than we originally thought. Brett thought it would be wise to teach the kids some technology lessons up front so that they would be better prepared for the research portion of the project. This proved to be very important once we got further along in the research.

Now we were ready to try out the states project using the adventure writing format. On our first attempt, we threw the kids into it and encouraged them as they swam along. We quickly discovered that the kids still needed some help to manage the task. Since then, Brett and I have worked to develop more scaffolding in anticipation of their needs. This is an enormous project for ten- and eleven-year-olds, and it can be overwhelming at first. They can definitely handle it, but they need to be shown how to do it.

First I divide the project into its two basic components: research and writing. These will come together later, but initially it's more effective to treat them separately. In this chapter, I'll show you how I've structured the research aspect of the project and give you some of the tools to help students succeed.

File Management

Each student has his or her own folder on the school server. As research begins, each student creates a digital research subfolder within that server folder, entitled "State Adventure Project." Then I show them how to create subfolders within their "State Adventure Project" folder to organize their materials for this project. They have one folder for images, one for notes and researched information (including WebQuests), and one for drafts of their adventure essay (which they'll use later). As the project gets rolling, students find these folders helpful in organizing their materials and often create new subfolders of their own as they become necessary.

WebQuests for Research

Although each student has his or her own state to research, they use a common WebQuest that I've created specifically for this purpose. (See pages 120–134 in Appendix A for a copy of this WebQuest packet. I've included this as a model. In all likelihood, you will want to create one of your own based on the specific content of your students' own research projects.) I show my students how to save the digital WebQuest files into their own computer folders so they can fill them in on their computers as they complete their research. The first section of the WebQuest includes five or six Web sites where students can find general information about their state (Grolier's online encyclopedia, for example). Next to each Web site, I give a brief description of the site and let students know what type of information they'll be able to find there. If a site requires a school password and login, I include it here so that students can research as independently as they'd like. Below this list of Web sites in the WebQuest packet is a place for students to record their research findings.

The second section of the WebQuest is devoted to images. Again, a list of useful Web sites is given that provides plenty of sources for photos to help kids with their projects. Images are a key part of this project, not only because they have been so effective in getting students to explore their writing in the first stages of the writing process (see Chapter 1, "Setting Descriptions"), but obviously because photos give the kids glimpses of what their state looks like. These are usually pictures of what they would see if they were actually traveling to these places, and often, as a result, kids find areas of research that they might otherwise have skipped over. As they discover useful images, the kids record the images' titles and URLs on a table in their WebQuest packet (see page 127 in Appendix A for a model). I also ask them to save the images directly into their computer folder so that they can bring them up later when they need to describe specific locations in their adventure stories.

In the final section of the WebQuest packet, students refer to a different set of Web sites, which I provide, to find more specific information about their state, such as local newspapers, weather, and road maps. The last part of this section asks students to choose three to five specific locations in their state they would like to visit. I provide a range so that it's manageable for all my students. These locations might be cities, historic monuments, national parks, or other major points of interest in each state. The kids find information and at least one picture for each location and, on their computers, enter it on the table provided in their digital packet (see pages 131–133 in Appendix A).

By combining all the different resources in their WebQuest packets and drawing information from them, kids will be well prepared and ready to dive into their writing projects. Each year I modify the WebQuest packet as Web sites change and new ones emerge. Sometimes my students find their own new Web sites to add to the list.

Digital Files Versus Paper

I used to have students write their researched information on a hard copy of the WebQuest packet. This year, however, I changed all the blank lines into text boxes, allowing the kids to type their answers right into their WebQuest packet. The boxes are expandable, so the kids aren't limited by the size of the text box. This eliminates many problems and makes the material more useful to the students later. They can access it from multiple locations, and they can add to it over the course of the entire project. Having it as a digital file also helps students keep their research organized. Most important, the digital files can be copied for backup; this diminishes the chances for research to be lost or misplaced, as often happens with hard copies.

Note: In Appendix A I've included the original version, which has lines for students to write on rather than text boxes, simply because it serves as a better model if it were to be used as a handout.

Bibliography

Included in the WebQuest packet is a blank bibliography table, which students can add to as they come across new resources (see page 134 in Appendix A). Again, it's helpful for students to put this in a computer file so they can copy and paste complex Web addresses directly into their bibliographies. In the past students would often skip one letter or character when transcribing an address and have to spend a great deal of time trying to find it again. In addition to all the Web sites listed for this project, we also use books, maps, and sometimes even interviews as sources. These, too, can be added to their bibliographies as the research is underway. At the end of the project, they have all their sources in one location, so creating a final bibliography is quick and easy.

Teaching Research Skills

Not all students have the same set of research skills coming into this project, so certain key skills need to be taught. They may be new for some and review for others, but I find it very useful to teach these lessons to the class early in the process, so that everyone can apply the skills and work more efficiently. I often teach these skills as mini-lessons, followed by a research session where students can practice. Mini-lessons usually include:

- Research ethics
  - The importance of citing sources and not plagiarizing
  - The importance of a bibliography
- Creating a bibliography
  - How to cite various types of resources
- Finding reliable sources and using multiple resources
- Use of WebQuests as part of the research process
- Note-taking skills and summarizing
- Image search
  - Image resolution
  - Finding URLs

✦ Web site navigation tools
✦ Use of search engines
    ✧ Safe search options
    ✧ Opening multiple tabs in a search

During the research process other ideas and problems often come up that warrant other mini-lessons. For example, one of my students recently found that it was easier to go back and forth between her research and her writing if she could see both windows at the same time by minimizing the documents. We stopped what we were doing and used the occasion to show the group how to create a "split screen" by minimizing the windows and displaying two documents or Web sites at once. For some students this was more convenient than clicking back and forth between tabs on the task bar.

There's a great sense of camaraderie among the kids as they all set out to search for knowledge about their respective states. When it's presented as a challenge and an opportunity to learn something new and share it with others, they realize that they're all in this together and they're eager to help one another. For example, students frequently come across new Web sites that may be useful to others, and they're eager to share them. One day Ben was looking for a restaurant in Philadelphia when he came across a great Web site that allows you to search for restaurants across the country. I stopped the class and had Ben demonstrate how to find and use the new Web site. The other kids were very appreciative, and Ben was proud of his contribution.

On another day I was showing students how to use Google Maps to find directions and travel times between two cities in their states. As the students began to work with it, Tyler discovered a camera icon in the driving directions. He clicked on it and was surprised to see that a photo of a Colorado highway appeared on his screen. I stopped the class once again and had him demonstrate for the other kids how to use the "street view" feature. Everyone began typing in their own street addresses or the school address to see street views of familiar areas. This tool quickly became a great opportunity to find images of specific areas in the states that they were researching. Just as quickly, the kids combined this with the "split screen," and soon they had their adventure essays open on the right side of the screens while they searched for images of specific locations on the left. When they found the image they wanted on the left, they could describe it in words in their essay on the right. One student's curiosity about an icon rapidly resulted in a whole classroom of enthusiastic researchers.

The task of research can be daunting for students, but it becomes manageable when it's broken into smaller sections with clear objectives and effective resources. Even with the wide range of abilities in my inclusion class, all my students are successful with this phase of the project. Once they complete their research, we are ready to begin planning the essay and looking for opportunities to join the two.

Chapter 7

The Adventure Essay

As the research portion comes to a close, the kids start to develop a greater understanding of their subject and invariably become interested in something they have found. This puts them in a perfect position to begin the essay itself. Maybe they've learned about an important historical figure; maybe they've come across a fascinating story that took place long ago in the state they're researching; maybe they found out about an incredible wilderness area they'd like to explore; but something always grabs their attention more than anything else. This becomes the catalyst for the whole adventure story. This newfound passion is what inspires them to take their collection of facts and turn them into something that they can be a part of. This is their jumping-off point—the transition from research to storytelling, from a hodgepodge of details to a cohesive narrative.

Once they're inspired, the writing comes easily. Unfortunately, it sometimes comes too easily, and the stories tend to drift, rudderless, from one scene to the next. The first time I tried the adventure essay, I didn't have students do enough planning. I was simply glad they were so motivated to write and didn't want to hold them back or stifle their creativity. I've since found that because the stories tend to be quite involved and lengthy, students need to do some essential planning up front. It's very difficult for them to plan once they're into their writing. Instead, up-front planning serves as a road map later on if they lose track of where they're headed and need guidance. I break it down here to highlight the essential components of this planning process.

Adventure Planning

- ✦ The Quest
  - ✧ Why are you going there? What do you hope to explore, learn, discover, reveal?
  - ✧ Why is this quest so important to you? Is this a worthy quest?
- ✦ Sequence of Locations and Transitions Between Locations
  - ✧ Where will you go on your adventure? In what order will you visit these places? Where will your adventure end?
  - ✧ Why do you go from one place to the next? What leads you on in your adventure?
- ✦ Travel Plans
  - ✧ How will you get from one place to another (maps, highways, forms of transportation, distances, travel times)?
  - ✧ Where will you stay along the way? Where will you eat?

The Quest

Planning can be done in any number of ways; the key is getting the students to think through their entire narrative so that it makes sense and comes together in the end. I usually begin this planning process with a few simple questions: *Why are you going to this state? What do you hope to explore, learn, discover, reveal?* We always follow this with the next logical questions: *Why is this quest so important to you? Is this a worthy quest?* I have the kids think about these questions and write answers to them so that they'll be able to clearly explain their adventure and why they undertook it.

At this point, it's important to have a class discussion about the quests the kids have chosen. We usually start by talking about what makes a good adventure. For example, the subject of the adventure has to be challenging, but not impossible. Is it worth the energy to travel to Colorado in search of a pine forest? Is it reasonable to look for a lost gold mine in a state that has no gold? Often the kids have great advice for each other and are able to strengthen their own ideas—and their conviction for their ideas—through this process. This is also a perfect time to help kids who are not as passionate about their ideas, and those whose ideas are clearly not going to work out. Every year when someone wants to drive across Tennessee in search of the ghost of Elvis, we end up discussing the difference between fantasy and adventure. As a group, we help the student come up with a similar, but perhaps more reasonable alternative.

Last year one of my students was completely stuck at this point. He had no idea what to write about. So we went back and looked at his research on the great state of Virginia. As we read through it together, he was overwhelmed by all the information. I asked him to close his notebook and just tell me what he remembered about Virginia. He immediately started talking about George Washington and Mount Vernon. He actually had learned quite a bit about this because it had been an area of interest for him for some time. He seemed to thoroughly enjoy talking about it, so we sat together for a while and, on the Internet, did a bit more research on George Washington. We even found copied excerpts from letters and a diary. Suddenly, he blurted out, "What if he had had another diary? What if it got lost during the American Revolution?"

"Great!" I said. "Now you're onto something!" Once you have an idea like that to work with, everything else falls into place.

We talked about what type of person might go looking for a lost diary—maybe a historian, maybe a professor, maybe even a treasure hunter. We pulled out our Virginia map and reopened his research notes. "In what areas of Virginia might you look for it? Where would you begin your search?" I asked. And he was off and running.

Many times, students will choose a subject for their adventure that relates to a personal interest. These kids have an advantage because they may have some background knowledge that they can combine with their research. I encourage everyone to do this, to look for something that they already know about or to find a topic that they are willing to invest time in researching further. If this is the case, the subject will continue to motivate them throughout the entire project. As a result, their projects usually turn out to be the best essays in the end.

A couple of years ago, I had a student named Klara who had always been fascinated by wolves. She chose Alaska so that she could learn more about wolves while exploring their natural habitat. Her quest was to spend a year in Alaska living with wolves and learning about their social structure. Her goal was to show that wolves are not the bloodthirsty creatures of fairy tales, but rather wonderful and intelligent animals that should be respected. It was a perfect project for her, and she learned a great deal in the process.

In 2005, shortly after Hurricane Katrina devastated New Orleans, Molly decided to study Louisiana for her state project. Her adventure centered on finding homes for the dogs that were abandoned or lost as a result of the storm. She found photos on the Internet and described the destruction that she saw as she traveled around the state in search of homes for these lost dogs. In her conclusion, when most students decide to return home to New York, she decided to stay in Louisiana and work for a volunteer agency rebuilding houses for the people who lost theirs. Through her research and her writing of this amazing essay, Molly was able to tap into something that was important to her and make it a virtual reality for herself through writing.

Again, the key is to help the kids find something to which they can connect, something that fascinates them, and ultimately something that they want to learn more about. If it's something that's interesting to me but not to them, it doesn't usually work because there's no intrinsic motivation in it. Before we can move forward, every student must have a quest that will work as an adventure story, but also one about which they are passionate.

Sequence of Locations and Transitions Between Locations

Next, I ask the students to think about where they will travel on their adventure. This helps with overall structure and pacing. *Where will you begin your search? Where will you go next? Where will your adventure end?* We look at our state maps and our research to answer these questions. I also have them explain why they have decided to go to these places and why they've chosen a particular sequence. They usually have good reasons for their choices, but if they don't, we go over their sequence together to try to come up with the best possible plan that fits with their research and works with their plans for the adventure story. This is a great time to teach students the need for an essay built on relevant ideas and information. All parts contribute to the whole, to the quest.

We always have a class discussion at this point to draw the kids' attention to a few important concepts. They need to understand that adventures are different from vacations. Although the adventurer may come upon a clue accidentally, he or she usually goes from one place to another for a reason. There's always something that leads the adventurer on to the next location. We talk about books we've read and come up with examples that demonstrate this. With this in mind, the kids go back to their planning and think and write about their transitions. *Why do you go from one place to the next? What leads you on in your adventure?* (See the Adventure Planning Page on pages 138–139 in Appendix A. I give the kids a hard copy of this form to fill in as they pore over their maps. Once they've finished, I put a digital copy of the template in their "State Adventure Projects" computer folders and have them type in the information. This helps the kids organize their thoughts, and it keeps the information from becoming lost.)

Planning really helps the kids by giving their narratives a structure. As always, if they want to change things later they can, but this gives them a place to start and a bit of scaffolding to keep them focused should they get lost later on in the adventure.

Travel Plans

The last step in the planning stage is more practical and offers a great way to teach the power of specific details in writing. I remind them of Pete's mantra, "Good writing is detailed writing."

I ask the kids to conduct some specific, travel-related research so that they will know exactly how they will make their journey. *How will you get from one place to another? Where will you stay? Where will you eat?* Using the Internet and road maps, they plan their travels from point A to point Z. In order for the journey to become believable to the writer and eventually the reader, the kids have to know the specifics: highway names, travel distances and times, and so on. They might choose different forms of transportation to make their trips more interesting. For example, one kid may decide to fly to the capital city of his state, rent a car at the airport, and then canoe down a river. Other kids may take trains or buses for their entire trip.

This portion of the planning usually requires some help from me, so I guide kids through a variety of Web sites, showing them how to find flights, train schedules, and rental cars as well as how to determine distances and travel times between locations. Maybe we'll go to the Web site for Southwest Airlines to plan for the flight, then to Avis to choose a rental car, to Amtrak to find a train schedule, and to Google Maps to find distances and travel times.

Finding hotels and restaurants is another important part of their pre-writing research. My only rule here is that the kids can't stay at chain hotels and they can't eat at chain restaurants. I find that the adventures tend to be more interesting if they stay at a locally owned bed and breakfast rather than a chain hotel that looks pretty much the same no matter where you are. The same goes for restaurants. When searching the Internet, the chains usually come up first, and the kids require a bit of guidance to steer them toward more locally owned, authentic places.

Oftentimes these places have their own Web sites that include interesting history about the establishment or the local area, as well as photos. For example, a bed and breakfast may be located in an old historic mansion, which the students can include in their stories. A few years back, I was conferencing with a student when I came to a beautiful description of her entering a bed and breakfast somewhere in Louisiana. She described the sounds of her heels clicking on the white marble and the chandelier glittering across the way. I asked her where she got this great image. "I'll show you," she said excitedly. She opened a Web site showing a magnificent old bed and breakfast, where she decided to stay one night during her journey through Louisiana.

The same is true for restaurants, cafes, and diners; frequently older, family-run places have the most interesting Web sites with personal stories of how the business was started (and maybe some great photos to illustrate those stories). Just to make it that much more believable for the students and, eventually, for the reader, I'll ask the kids to tell me what they're eating along the way; most Web sites for restaurants and diners include a menu. "Oh, I'll have the Hungry Man's No. 2, over easy with whole-wheat toast and a side of corned beef hash, please."

Making these virtual journeys real for the kids is what keeps them going. At first they think I'm crazy when I ask them to give me so many details, but soon they see that it's possible, and fun, to find out almost anything on the Internet. When a kid says to me, "Well, I'm not going to stay in a hotel, I'm going to camp out by a stream and just fish for my dinner." Great, I say, So show me on the map where you plan to camp. How will you get there? How far will you have to hike? What's the name of the stream where you'll pitch your tent? What kinds of fish live in that stream? These types of questions drive them mad, but at the same time they love the challenge. In the end, it's the answers to these specific questions that will take a dull and lifeless story and turn it into an authentic and vibrant journey.

The students compile and organize all the information gathered during this adventure-planning phase in their adventure notebooks or computer files for use in their adventure essays. This includes various personal notes, train schedules, flight information, hand-sketched maps, trail maps, names and addresses of diners and hotels, photos and menus from restaurants, highway names and printouts from Google Maps—whatever they will need to write their way from one place to another across their respective states.

Mentor Texts

✦ Reasons for Referring to Mentor Texts
  ✧ To understand the writer's craft
  ✧ To establish the basic elements of the genre
  ✧ To reinforce a concept by providing examples of how it is done in writing

✦ Adventure Writing Examples
   ✧ Peter Lourie—Uses elements of the adventure model
   ✧ Bill Bryson—Uses humor and dialogue to engage the reader and advance the story
   ✧ Henry Shukman—Paints a picture with words to establish setting prior to inviting in the character (see example on pages 77–78)
   ✧ Craig Childs—Continually discovers history throughout the journey
   ✧ Tom Claytor—Blends factual information and storytelling (see example on page 79)

Reasons for Referring to Mentor Texts

I should explain what I mean by "mentor text." Generally, the term refers to books that are used in their entirety to serve as a model. I use books in this way too; however, I find that sometimes I only need a great paragraph or two to quickly demonstrate a point. I refer to these paragraphs as mentor texts as well, because they serve the same purpose in teaching. Sometimes I read the text aloud just so that students can hear how it flows. Other times, when I want to dissect the text a bit more, I'll read it aloud, but also project the words on the whiteboard. This allows the kids to follow along with the analysis and to point things out that I may have missed. If I want them to be able to refer back to the text repeatedly, I'll make copies to hand out after the lesson.

However you do it, reading and analyzing the writing of others is an important part of the teaching of writing. I use mentor texts in preparation for most writing projects, but also during the writing process itself. Both have the power to really enhance student writing because the students see the mechanics, the inner workings, of great writing and they begin to see ways to apply those mechanics to their own work. Maybe it's because writing is so seemingly complex, or maybe it's because in discussing the craft of writing we're often dealing with concepts that are abstract for kids, but having clear examples of strong writing is very effective in helping students become better writers.

Adventure Writing Examples

In preparing for the adventure essay, we read Peter Lourie's *The Lost Treasure of Captain Kidd*, a short, well-crafted adventure novel. As we go through the book, I help the kids see that it's more than just a great story; it's also a model for a well-composed adventure. By analyzing the writing (its plot structure, transitions, character development, dialogue, and setting) the kids begin to see the story from the writer's perspective as well as the reader's. They come to understand why the author chose to craft the story the way he did. And that leads them to becoming better writers because bit by bit they become conscious writers.

For example, early on in their reading of this story, when we talk about characters, I ask the kids why they think the author chose Alex, the level-headed kid, to be the narrator and Killian, the reckless and semicrazy kid, to be the sidekick rather than the other way around. By talking about it and looking at it from the writer's point of view, we realize that the Pete did it intentionally; he probably knew, consciously or subconsciously, that most readers would identify with the more level-headed character and thereby become engaged in the story. At the same time, the writer knew that there needed to be a somewhat crazy character in the story, too, or nothing all that exciting was going to happen. The crazy character adds complexity and raises the stakes for the level-headed character. In fact, the crazy guy pushes Alex deeper and deeper into trouble as he drives the plot to an exciting finish.

I'm oversimplifying it a bit here, but these are the kinds of discussions that lead to good writing because they lead to good thinking. By examining each chapter, each event, each step in the story, we begin to get inside the writer's mind and understand that everything that happens in a story is based on a decision made by the author. Then, when the students transition to the role of adventure writers, I continually refer back to this novel and remind them that they need to make these types of conscious decisions to engage readers in their own stories as well. This connection between reading and writing is invaluable to the young writers because it helps them look at writing from a new perspective.

We've used Pete's *The Lost Treasure of Captain Kidd* in another way as well. Before we start reading the novel, we have a class brainstorming session in which we define adventure writing. We then come up with traits that distinguish it from other genres. We make a list of these traits, which I refer to as the "Elements of Adventure" (see pages 136–137 in Appendix A). In developing this list, we discuss both fiction and nonfiction adventure stories, and we discover that the basic elements are really the same in both. This discovery is important to the kids as they begin to think through their own adventure narratives because, since they themselves won't travel to these places during the school year, or maybe ever, their creations will necessarily be a conscious weave of nonfiction and fiction elements.

Throughout the reading of *The Lost Treasure of Captain Kidd*, I have students refer to this list over and over again, modifying it when necessary. Whenever we add a new adventure element, we inevitably find concrete examples from the text to illustrate it.

Mentor texts can also be effective during the writing process itself. I like to introduce new ideas for the kids to think about when they reach certain points in their essays. Of course I could explain a particular idea, but having samples of great writing right in front of them shows the kids how these elements of the craft can actually work. Writing samples help bridge the gap between concept and reality—an important distinction that I continually emphasize. It's more effective to show an idea through the use of concrete and specific details than it is to tell something using generalized or abstract concepts.

For instance, I might explain to the kids that they can include humor in their dialogue to make it more believable and to help draw in the reader; sometimes it's important to be able to laugh at yourself when you're on an adventure. Many kids will hear this and understand the concept, but still not really know how to accomplish it in their own writing. But reading a short, hilarious passage from Bill Bryson's *A Walk in the Woods* offers them a concrete example of what I'm talking about. Instantly they have a picture of what they can choose to do in their own writing. Sometimes it's useful to read a few different samples to show a variety of ways in which an idea can be presented to the reader.

As this project has developed over the years, I've relied more and more on samples of writing to help explain some of the big ideas. Last year when my students were getting to a point where they wanted to introduce a character in their essays, I read them a beautiful passage from Henry Shukman's *The Lost City*. The writer paints a scene with amazingly detailed descriptions, then has the character emerge from the scene. He begins by describing the landscape at the western foot of the Peruvian Andes—the dull gray ocean, the lifeless strip of desert crossed by two rivers. It's done so gracefully that I wouldn't do it justice if I tried to explain it without reading his actual words to the students:

> *Just north of the northern river a dirt track forged straight at the mountains then petered out in a path which soon forked and lost itself among the rocks of the foothills. Farmers used the track, piling ancient pickups with towers of bananas and pineapples among which they perched, struggling to keep the loads from tumbling as they swayed down to market.*

Late on a Thursday afternoon toward the end of the garua season an empty truck made its way up the track. From above, all you saw was a plume of dust travelling along with a kind of self-absorbed determination, as if an animal were furiously burrowing its way just under the surface, an invisible point churning up a wake of dust. Then a little black dot showed at the front of the cloud, trembling in the distance. It grew slowly, coming straight up the hill; the only moving thing in the landscape. Then it stopped. It seemed to grow broader. A tiny human figure emerged. Then, as if in slow motion, the truck turned off the path, described a large lazy circle, rocked back onto the track facing the opposite way, and trundled back in the direction of the distant ocean.

The man who had got out pulled on a rucksack and took a step to balance himself. He was a young man who stood still, watching the truck drive away. (Shukman 2008, 4–5)

Of course, this is just a snippet from a three-hundred-page novel, but in the couple of minutes that it takes to read the passage the students get a brilliant example of what is possible to accomplish at this point in their own essays; namely, using setting to introduce, reflect, or emphasize a character. Shukman makes certain choices in sentence structure, syntax, and diction (take a look at those powerful action verbs such as "forged," "petered out," and "forked" or strong images such as "ancient pickups with towers of bananas and pineapples") that are invaluable for young writers to see. These are choices that every writer can make. With exposure to good writing, kids begin to realize that they, too, are the masters of their own writing; they, too, have choices to make.

Later on in the writing process, when the kids are starting to weave more and more history into their essays, I may read a bit from Craig Childs' *House of Rain*. In this amazing work of nonfiction, Childs takes a journey on foot across much of the Four Corners region of the Southwest in search of clues about the ancient civilization of the Anasazi. The entire book is a blend of the author's personal experience coupled with historical information. The two are woven so expertly that it reads like a novel.

In addition to books, I sometimes look online to find pieces of text that I can read to my kids to exemplify a point made in class. A few years ago I found a series of letters that a young traveler had posted on the Internet. The well-written letters detailed his experiences traveling through India. Finding them was like stumbling on an exquisite secret diary, and I shared them with my students to show them the sense of wonderment that can work its way into the writing of a good travel writer.

On another occasion, when I was looking for material to use as a mentor text, my friend Brett Adams told me about Tom Claytor and his incredible journey around the world in a bush plane. We looked him up and found not only his Web site but archives of his travel journals. We read bits of many of his journals aloud to show the kids how to successfully combine storytelling and factual information about a specific location. Hearing about his adventures inspires my students to work even harder to make their stories as realistic as his.

Here's an excerpt from one of Claytor's journal entries.

11 Jun 1996—Diego-Suarez, Madagascar
It is still raining in Maroantsetra. I take off and climb into the mist. A swollen river snaking through the jungle disappears, and I am surrounded by clouds. I had watched the rain for the previous several days. It always stopped in the afternoon, and then as the sun set, the sky would be orange in a way that said that it was clear to the west. You can tell when you are near the top of the clouds, because the white around you becomes brilliant from the sun's light filtering through. After 30 minutes, the clouds are behind me. I am looking for a small town called Bealanana. It is in the highlands, and it is near the Tsaratanana Massif.

The high country beneath me is jagged and orange. Off in the distance, I can see a lush green valley of rice fields. To the north, the Massif rises up and down through thick bamboo jungle to the alpine summit of Maromokotro. It makes me feel a little strange inside, because I know this place.

I remember, down below, that mysterious lake. It had looked like a lush flat field. I was told to walk carefully. The vegetation on its surface was so thick that it supported me in a mysterious way—like walking on a waterbed. Halfway across, I had to test to see if this was so. I jumped, and then I jumped again harder; the vegetation gave way, and I immediately slid in up to the pack on my back. My feet were dangling in clear empty water . . .

These are just a few of the endless possibilities for mentor texts. I've chosen these because I enjoy reading them and because they work for me and for my students as poignant teaching examples during the writing of the adventure essay. I mention them only to demonstrate how I've used them in class, and I realize that all teachers choose books that are pertinent to their own needs and tastes, and to their own students. I usually discover the best samples unintentionally. I'll be reading a novel when all of sudden a description or a bit of dialogue or an interesting character will jump out from the lines around it. Later, in class, I might remember that beautiful passage that resonated with me as I'm teaching writing. So I go back and try to find the page or paragraph to share with my students the following lesson. Over the years I've gathered many samples like this, and I can continue to add to my collection as I go.

Putting It All Together

+ Step 1: Establishing the Setting
+ Step 2: Getting There
+ Step 3: Defining the Quest
+ Step 4: Developing Characters
+ Step 5: Diving into the Adventure
  ✧ Making Time for Conferencing
  ✧ Making Modifications
+ Step 6: Completing the Project
  ✧ Resolution
  ✧ Reflection

As mentioned earlier, I learned another thing from my first attempts at teaching the adventure essay: the process is difficult to manage (both for the kids and for me) if the adventure isn't broken into smaller sections. It doesn't matter exactly how the writing is sectioned, but it does need to be sectioned into manageable chunks. Without applying some organizing principles, the stories tend to ramble on. Initially I worried that dividing a story into sections might diminish the kids' creativity by overly formatting it for them. I found, though, that they're actually more creative working under some sort of structure; it allows them to focus on the content and not be distracted by trying to figure out a format of their own. Eventually all the sections will be revised with the addition of transitions to make the final essay flow seamlessly, so they can use this revision time to work more on the logic of their writing—before their final drafts. As they get older, they'll be able to work their way through a lengthy essay on their own, but for ten-year-olds, it's advantageous to help them with the structure of their pieces.

Step 1: Establishing the Setting

We start out with the setting. This helps draw the reader into the scene right away before the storytelling begins. Here too, I learned through trial and error. Our first adventure essays were much heavier on action and much lighter on details and descriptions. We soon discovered that it was difficult for the reader to engage in the story when the setting wasn't yet established.

After choosing a location where they'd like to start their adventures, the kids go to the Internet and find a photo of the place. Maybe it's sunrise at the Grand Canyon, a cool autumn day in the Cascade Mountains, or nighttime along Chicago's Lakeside Drive. I leave this up to the kids to choose, but require that they each pick a real location from the state they've researched that they can write about with some authority. With the images displayed on their computer screens, they begin writing a description of the scene. (See page 140 in Appendix A for a handout to accompany this section of the writing project, with student samples on pages 141–142.)

I remind the kids to use sensory descriptors so that the reader can fully visualize the scene, and imagine himself a part of it. Klara wrote an impressive essay about her virtual journey to Alaska, where she spent a year living with wolves. Her opening scene is short and simple, but it helps the reader by establishing the setting right off the bat.

> The engine of the jet I am in hums as we fly over Juneau. I look down into the inky waters of the harbor and see a large cruise ship heading towards the city. Juneau is the capital city of Alaska but it is a very modest-sized city. It looks to me like the entire population of Juneau could squeeze onto the cruise ship heading towards the harbor. Surrounding the city is a thick forest of pine trees, making Juneau look like an island of civilization in an endless sea of wilderness. And that is pretty much what Juneau is.

Ben created an equally impressive but completely different essay about digging up his past as he makes archaeological discoveries about his Native American ancestors. His adventure begins at the Museum of the American Indian in Washington, D.C., and takes him all the way to an archaeological site in Missouri.

> I'm blinded by the light as it reflects off the windows of an enormous building. The snake-like roof towers over me as I look up. I can hear small trees behind me rustling in the light breeze. The oddly shaped structure in front of me makes me feel like it does not belong here . . .
>
> As I stretch my legs, I remember the journey . . .

Step 2: Getting There

Next I ask my students to go back in time and describe how they arrived at this place. This idea came up in a class discussion about adventure writing. We had been reading adventure stories and looking for common traits in the structure of the narratives. One kid noticed that in several of the stories the setting description is followed by a flashback describing how the character came to this location. We tried it, and it worked well. (See page 143 for a handout with further explanation for the students.)

A clear transition is necessary so that the reader understands that the narrative is switching to past tense for a brief moment. I read examples to the kids to help them grasp the concept before they try it on their own.

They generally want to include too many details at this point. I encourage them to go easy on the details here so the reader doesn't forget where he's headed and remind them that in a well-built essay, nothing is extraneous. (Good writing is indeed detailed, but too many details can weigh down a good story—and even sink it.) There's a tricky balance that is difficult to achieve, and I'm not sure that I always get it right. Initially, kids include far too few details in their stories. Later, once they learn how to incorporate details, they tend to overdo it. Once they get the hang of it, they enjoy adding details, and I'm reluctant at first to spoil their enthusiasm. In the ideal situation, we would have all the time in the world to go back and look over the entire essay for extraneous facts and ensure that all information is crucial to the thesis, but truthfully, it doesn't always happen to the extent that it should.

Klara's essay describes the events that led up to her arrival in Alaska. In this case, some of the details are extraneous, but they don't slow the essay down too drastically, so I decide not to point them out.

It had taken me seven hours and forty minutes to get here, but it felt like more because I went through four time zones . . . I had to go to the Albany International Airport to get on an American Airlines flight that was leaving at 6:20 am. I arrived at Chicago at 7:40 in the morning. Then I had to wait 50 minutes until my next flight left. During that time I was able to go down to the baggage area and check on the dogs, who were doing well but looked a bit bored. Then it was time to board my next plane which was also an American Airlines. By now it was about 8:35 am. From there I flew to Seattle. I arrived there at about 11:00 am. My next flight was leaving at about 1:20 pm, so I had a few hours to wait. In that space of time, I was actually able to buy Hurricane from a local pound who I had contacted earlier. Then it was on to Juneau on Alaskan Airlines. Finally, I arrived at Juneau at 2:50 pm. To make a long story short, I had a very busy day.

Ben's journey was more complex and required a great deal more planning. He told me that he really couldn't go directly to his state (Missouri) because he needed to first get some information in Washington, D.C., which would then lead him to Missouri. "Fine," I said, "Let's get a U.S. map and plan your route." Early in his essay, Ben explains his circuitous trip, which eventually takes him to Missouri. Again, there's definitely some extraneous material here (details, details, details), but it's still effective as a means of showing the reader how he arrived at his destination:

I had driven from my hometown, Burnt Hills, NY, toward D.C. in an Enterprise rental car. After driving for 4 and one half hours, my stomach began to growl so I decided to stop in Philadelphia. As I stopped at a light on South Street, I noticed the rows of four story buildings surrounding me like a tunnel. People were weaving in and out of traffic as the light became green. I turned on to 9th Street and one restaurant caught my eye, Geno's Steaks. I parked the car, entered the building and smelled a strong aroma of onions and grease. I ordered their famous Philly cheese steak sandwich and was surprised by how quickly a massive hot, steamy masterpiece appeared before my eyes.

When I sat down and started to eat that monster of a sandwich, I saw a flier in front of me on a corkboard that said, "Geno's Steaks was first started by Joe Vento back in 1966. He had gotten the idea from his father that already made a cheese steak restaurant back in the early 1940's named Jim's Steaks. Joe started Geno's Steaks with only $6.00, 2 boxes of steaks, and some hot dogs." After reading that flier, I demolished the rest of my giant cheese steak. I decided to move on to Washington D.C.

For the next 2 hours and 38 minutes I drove on 611 S to I–95 S to arrive in Washington, D.C. I made my way south on 9th street and took a right on Lenfant Plaza SW to get me to the oddly shaped museum.

> The warm afternoon sun was beating on the back of my neck as I
> stepped into the Museum of the American Indian. It was as if I left modern
> civilization and was instantly surrounded by artifacts from the past . . .

Step 3: Defining the Quest

This is where the real meat of the story begins—where the reader learns why
we're there. Once you've created the setting and explained how you got
there, the next logical questions are, "So why did you go there?" and "Who
are you?" These questions should become clear as the kids complete this
section of their essays. (See page 144 in Appendix A for a handout with further details for students.)

Some of the planning that the kids did beforehand comes into play here.
Most of them know the material by heart, but I always encourage them to go
back and look at their notes before starting this section. I ask them to
include two major points in writing this section: (1) the writer's purpose for
traveling to the given state (the quest, the mission, the goal of the adventure), and (2) a description of who the narrator is in the story and the role he
or she will play.

Although most students write their essays in the first-person narrative
form, I tell them they can change their identity for the sake of the story. One
student may choose to become a disgruntled old treasure hunter looking for
a lost mine in northern California, while another might choose to become a
biology student completing her graduate studies on the endangered animals
of Montana. This is the fictional part that is essential to the story. Since these
are virtual journeys rather than real ones, I have to allow them this leeway in
order to make the essays believable and powerful. Pete always says, "Write
about what you know." And my students really do know a lot now that
they've explored so much on the Internet. The researched information,
which becomes the content of the essay, must be factual; however, in order
to make it believable, the students may need to fictionalize their characters.
It's this blend of fiction and nonfiction that makes these virtual adventures
work so well.

For example, last year in Tyler's Colorado adventure, he was an archaeologist who had traveled there to discover the reason for the decline of the
Anasazi civilization some six or seven hundred years ago. Tyler, of course, was
just a ten-year-old kid from New York, but in the story he took on another per-
sona—that of an archaeologist. Nevertheless, the information about Colorado
and about the Anasazi, which he wove into his story, was all factual.

Klara explains why she has gone to Alaska and what she hopes to do there. The "why" is part of her backstory, while the "hope to do" is essential to her quest. This is where character meets thesis:

I am sitting in my room at the Juneau Airport Travel Lodge Hotel. The dogs are very happy to be in open space again because I got permission from the hotel manager to allow them out of their crates. I am thinking about all of the amazing things I'll be doing this year. I'll be spending one year traveling around Alaska getting to know several different wolf packs! My aim is to prove to everyone that wolves are not the vicious creatures that they know from storybooks, but in fact, compassionate, respectful and intelligent creatures. If there's anywhere I can find an abundance of wolves—it's Alaska. My field research will concentrate on wolf behavior and the relationship dynamics between wolves in a pack. National Geographic has agreed to fund my research and will publish my findings in their magazine. This is like a dream come true for me because I've been a wolf lover since I was a fourth grader. I have spent four years in college studying animal psychology. Now I will be able to share my love of wolves with the public! I feel like I'm in heaven already!

Ben handled this a bit differently in his essay. Since he had to stop in Washington on his way to Missouri, he decided that his quest should be explained to the reader while he's still in Washington. It made good sense to do it this way. Here you can see how this first leg of the trip leads to the next.

It is a dream come true to be here. Since graduating from The University of North Carolina four years ago, I have been tracing my family tree. My Grandfather had long ago told me stories of our family's rich American Indian heritage. Until now, simply reading about the lives and history of the Missouri Indians was the closest I had come. But now artifacts from my ancestors were everywhere. It took me a while, but now I could see them here in front of me.

I was drawn to a case with some of the most interesting pieces of history. In front of me stood a plaque that explained that the items were found near Bluff Dwellers Cave in Noel, Missouri. The Browning family discovered the artifacts when they bought a house that was over the cave. During the excavation, the discovery was made. After I read the article, I decided to ask a museum worker more about the Missouri Indians. He provided me with a list of national experts on file at the museum. I scanned the list and saw the name Alex W. Barker, professor at The University of Missouri and an expert on American archeology. I knew to learn more I would need to get closer to where my ancestors lived and to see what Alex Barker could tell me. Before I could think about leaving for St. Louis, I needed to see all I could of the museum and get a good night's sleep.

I checked into the Intown Uptown Inn on 14th St. in Washington D.C. and scheduled my flight to St. Louis on United Airlines out of Dulles International Airport. I spent a comfortable night in the "Room with a View" suite, the most expensive room in the Inn! The next morning I jumped onto flight number 8021 at 8:40. I flew for 2 hours and 30 minutes before arriving in St. Louis. We touched down and the pilot said "Welcome to St. Louis. The current time is 10:08." I remembered to change my watch because I was now in the central time zone. It was a smooth flight and I was excited for the next step in my journey . . .

Step 4: Developing Characters

As Pete always says, "The best thing about traveling is meeting interesting new people." In class discussions during the planning stage we often talk about the interesting characters that emerge in adventure stories, both fictional and nonfictional. To make the essays more believable and more entertaining, I ask my students to introduce at least one interesting character into the story.

This has advantages for the students. It allows them to include dialogue and also gives them an opportunity to have their narrator ask questions that can be answered by the other character(s). This interaction gives the students an effective means of weaving factual information into the essay. For this reason, I encourage the kids to create several characters with whom they come in contact along their journey. Some students choose to create a single character who acts as a travel partner throughout the trip. In any case, having additional characters adds to the storytelling component, and it gives the writer a chance to incorporate information that may seem awkward if introduced through the narrator alone. The information being discussed could be something very complex, like a conversation between the narrator and a biology professor about the leading causes of extinction in a specific animal population.

It might also be something as simple as finding one's way from point A to point B. For example, if the main character is trying to get from one place to another, and has written something like, "So I headed north on highway 84 until I came into the town of Abiquiu. On the right there was a sign pointing the way to Georgia O'Keefe's Ghost Ranch," a more interesting alternative might be for the writer to decide to have the main character stop for breakfast at a diner and ask the waitress, "So can you tell me how to get to Ghost Ranch?" "Sure thing," she says, "Just hang a right out of the parkin' lot and you'll be on highway 84 headin' north. Just follow along for about twenty miles until you come to Abiquiu. You'll see signs from there. What a place it is too! Some say it's haunted!"

In *The Lost Treasure of Captain Kidd*, Pete uses dialogue between the two main characters to teach the reader about the history of Captain Kidd. In fact, much of the historical background is relayed to the reader through this casual dialogue between friends. It's a very effective technique because it allows the writer to share factual information that comes across naturally and at the same time helps bring into focus the tension that is growing between the two boys.

Here's a scene near the beginning of the book. As Killian, the treasure hunter, and Alex, his partner who lacks historical knowledge, make their way across the great Hudson River on a small motorboat, Killian reminds Alex about a few important historical details of Captain Kidd's life:

"Well, you remember Clermont, don't you? That's Livingston's old estate." [said Killian]

"Livingston?"

"Don't you remember anything??? He's the guy who hired Kidd to become a pirate."

"Yeah, yeah, I know, I know." I remembered the name Clermont, but I was fuzzy on exactly who Livingston was."

Killian shook his head, looking as if he might stomp off in one of his fits again. Problem was, there was nowhere to stomp. He'd have to swim.

I felt better when his voice grew softer. I could see he was trying to be patient.

"Listen, Alex, you're never going to find anything unless you know history. History is everything." (Lourie 2000a, 19)

Reading through Pete's nonfiction books for other examples, I found many interesting characters in each book who play some role in telling the story of his adventures. So it's not only helpful to bring in other characters, but it's the way adventures usually happen in the real world, so it makes it more believable.

Chris, whose essay took him treasure hunting in Washington State, had fun with this character development piece. In his essay he runs into an old treasure hunter with whom he eventually joins up. But in his first meeting with this guy, you get an interesting image of the crazy old man.

While walking to his house I noticed an old man. The man had a tight face as if he had smelled raw fish. His face was soiled with dirt and he had dark rings around his eyes, as if he were up all night. His eyes were a soulless pale blue color. The man had a scraggily black beard with braids shooting out of his face in every direction. The beard connected to his wavy black hair just above his ears. He wore a sailor hat with a black anchor on it. He also had a stretched out old shirt with coffee stains all over it.

"What do you want boy," he barked. "I ain't got all day and I'm sure not gonna waste all my time hav'in you gawk at me."

"Well?"

Katie, who explores Pennsylvania in search of a lost diary belonging to Ben Franklin, travels to an Amish community in search of answers. She meets people from the community during a barn raising and begins to ask questions. In the process, the reader is introduced to some interesting new characters as well, one old guy in particular.

The first couple of people don't know him, but when I ask the third person, his eyes light up. "Jon Bachus! Why he was my uncle. Uncle Jon." The man looks like he is in his mid-eighties. He doesn't have any hair on his head, but his beard definitely makes up for that! It goes three-quarters of the way down his chest. I have never seen a beard so long in all my life (with the exception of Santa Claus!!!) "So why do you want to know?"

"I'm looking for the lost invention of Benjamin Franklin, and I was told relatives of his would know a lot about Franklin, just like he did."

"Boy is that true! I'll betcha I know more about him than Ol' Uncle Jon did!"

"Can you tell me about him? Ya know, like about how people found his diaries and other important information so I can find the diary with the lost invention?"

Every kid's essay is unique, so there's no right or wrong way to introduce characters, but I encourage them all to think about characters and find a way to include some in their essays. And I encourage them to think about how these characters contribute to the overall goal of the narrative, to the thesis. If the characters aren't relevant, they should be left out.

Where in the essay the character(s) appears is up to each individual student, but drawing attention to the development of characters early on in the process helps avoid the problem of characters who lack sufficient description. (For a handout designed to get your students thinking about characters, see page 145 in Appendix A.)

Before beginning work on the next section we go back and study our prewriting notes, specifically the notes on sequence of locations and transitions. If a student wants to make changes to his original plans, I encourage him to do so before beginning to write this section. Here they will refer to their notes almost like an outline, so I find that the kids' notes are most useful if they're accurate and updated.

Step 5: Diving into the Adventure

Now the adventure is underway. We know how the main character arrived at his or her destination; we know what he or she hopes to discover there; we have a plan for how the discovery will unfold; we even have a few interesting characters who will emerge in different parts of the story. So now it's time to take off and begin traveling around the state in search of the lost diary, the sought-after treasure, the quest for knowledge, or whatever it is they're seeking.

Ben begins this section with a visit to an archaeology professor at a local university.

I clear my thoughts as I anxiously grab my bags and pick up my rental car . . . Once I load my bags in the trunk, I quickly punch, 801 E Walnut St. Columbia, Missouri into my GPS. This is the campus where Alex's lab is. Driving on Lambert International Boulevard is interesting because of the fading airport in the distance. . . .

My heart begins to race when I can finally see the University on College Avenue. It feels familiar being on a campus again, just like a college student. I park my car and start walking toward the building of science and archeology. The doors creak when I push them open. I get a couple of odd looking stares when I walk down the hall.

Katie begins this portion of the journey by heading to a university library to do some much-needed research.

It is 9:00 when my alarm goes off, and I crawl out of bed to take a shower. I am lucky, considering the University of Pennsylvania is only eight minutes away. Wanting to be as prepared as possible, I grab my notebook and a pencil and my purse with extra pencils and pens, water, a few snacks, money, my guidebook, and a small map. Catching a taxi is exceptionally easy this morning, since it is a Sunday and nobody has to go to work; well, except for me, of course.

Klara's Alaskan adventure begins quite differently, by heading into the wilderness with her dog team in search of a wolf pack.

The sky was overcast and it rained most of the time. The further north we got, the more mountainous it became. Aurora passed the time by sitting in the front seat and howling. Fortunately, no one else joined her. Finally, we arrived at Whale Pass. It was a small town and, once again, it was surrounded by forest. We made a quick stop at the local food store and then we were off. We drove down a winding dirt road that was surrounded by misty mountains covered in (what else?) dense forest. I heard a noise that sounded like a cross between a growl, a yawn and a whine. Windy was in the front seat this time, and once in a while she makes that strange noise that I call a "growl-yawn."

We arrived at a U-shaped valley, and I decided that it would be a good place to set up camp. When I let the dogs out of the car, they ran around gleefully, leaving tracks in the dirt road. But then I noticed some fresh canine tracks that I'm sure didn't belong to the dogs. There was only one other animal they could belong to. They were wolf tracks! And there were five sets of them! Wow, I sure did choose the right place to stop! I picked up my bags and set off into the valley, thinking happily to myself that every step I took led me deeper into wolf country.

As the kids progress through this section of their essay, I check in with them daily to help with all sorts of details, from finding a restaurant online, to figuring out how long it'll take to drive from point A to point B, to finding the best way to weave the relevant details of their research into their tales of adventure.

At this point, I still tend to let them keep a few more details than they really need in their drafts. Teaching them the importance of detail is one of my major focuses now. As I work with them I ask, How does this detail help your narrative? Can we leave it out? Is it essential? With other kids I may ask, Can we find more details to explain this part more effectively? Invariably some students have too much detail while others lack specifics. Finding the perfect balance within each essay is an essential and ongoing task. By now all students have completely diverged in different directions, so continually checking in and keeping up to date with their progress is crucial.

This part of the process, where much of the action is introduced, is the most significant in terms of travel within the state. For that reason, it's naturally the best opportunity for students to integrate their state research into the fabric of the narrative. Through a combination of mini-lessons, quick examples, and individual writing conferences, we look for ways to incorporate background information so that it's more than just a fabricated narrative—it's a realistic journey backed up by researched material. Initially students are frustrated with this because they'd rather write without worrying about how to make it more realistic, but with some help and guidance they come to see it not only as interesting but also as a fun challenge. They can see that this comprehensive approach adds depth to their stories and brings out their own expertise on the subject.

Ben really enjoyed the challenge and found many ways to weave his research into his adventure. As he arrives in St. Louis he describes the scene before diving into the events that lead him on in his journey:

> I quickly notice the warm summer air as I step out of the plane in St. Louis. A blinking billboard welcomes me at the gate and reads, 77 degrees, which is an average for this time of year. I can already feel sweat rolling down my cheek as I make my way to the baggage claim. All around me are reminders that St. Louis is one of the major economic centers in Missouri. There are advertisements for Pfizer Pharmaceuticals and Emerson Electric. I remember that in a book that I read, it said that St. Louis was founded by French fur traders from New Orleans, Louisiana in 1764. They named the city after Louis IX, a king of France during the 1200s, who was later declared a saint. The city was built on Spanish territory 18 miles south of where the Missouri and Mississippi Rivers meet . . . There is one of the most visited attractions in Missouri, the 630 foot tall, St. Louis Arch designed by Eero Saarinen and one of the most recognizable sights.

This blending of narrative writing with factual information is what becomes the most difficult—and the most inspiring—for the kids. It's usually challenging initially because they've never done anything like this before. Once they get the hang of it, they tend to do it inconsistently: they'll include too much information and slow the story down, or have trouble distinguishing between pertinent and erroneous information. But ultimately the challenge of weaving narrative with researched information enables them to see how details can enrich writing. And as they practice and struggle to get it right, they learn many lessons about the craft of writing.

Pete always seems to have a great balance in his nonfiction. As you follow him on his travels and discoveries, you're captivated by the narrative and the factual information simultaneously. So I asked him how he achieves this balance, telling the story of his experience in a place while also teaching us about the details of the place.

I try to convey to writing students that from the moment they come up with an idea, a thesis, a passionate quest of their own, to the moment the essay is handed in, absolutely nothing is set in stone. Anything can be changed at any moment. As you write, the story remains organic. You learn what it is you want to say, and how you might add bits and pieces here and there in order to fortify your main topic. I call this *layering*, because it's similar to what a painter might add to his canvas as he paints day after day. As the light shifts and colors change, artistic decisions are made. Always working toward one goal—making the best narrative possible.

Recently I was working on a book about an Arctic whale scientist who works with the Iñupiaq Eskimos on the North Slope of Alaska. I had done a pretty good job capturing the setting, that wild sea ice where the Eskimos bring in the whales in the spring. And I think I'd done a pretty good job, too, of creating a distinct character in the subject of my profile, Craig George, son of children's author Jean Craighead George. But on one of my early drafts, my editor at Houghton Mifflin pointed out that since this book was a Scientist in the Field Series book, I might need to add a little more science. I looked over the draft and suddenly saw that she was right. I was heavy on character, on cultural setting, on the Arctic beauty, and rather light on the actual science that Craig conducted when he went out on the ice with the People of the Whale to collect samples from whales that the Eskimos were hunting. I also needed to weave in this science throughout the text and not in a few isolated chunks. So I went back to work, and came up with some nice touches, I think. I hope. In fact, I had to reorder large sections of the book in order to make this happen. So I couldn't be afraid to throw things to the wind and start afresh. Young writers often hang on too dearly to their early drafts that might not be going in a productive, I should say effective, path.

Once a student in your fifth-grade class has written a first draft, for instance, you might help the writer see that perhaps the historical underpinnings aren't quite strong enough to make a forceful argument. So you can encourage such a writer at that moment to go back and layer in the relevant history. Or perhaps in another essay by a different student the element of a personal point of view is not personal enough. So you help the writer to think deeply about how he or she feels about the subject and then layer in this feeling. Or maybe a student sees all nonfiction as a simple sequence of events, a sort of boring laundry list of reportable facts and figures that lead nowhere— this student really and truly needs to work on the layering, the nuance, of personal commitment.

By layering I do not mean "coating." I'm talking more about the layers in a lasagna, built-in stuff, without which there is no food, no essay. I'm talking about the hints of color spread throughout the book that might be added after a first or second draft and that now contribute to the overall beauty of the tapestry, the silver-blue theme. I'm talking about more science. It could be layers of setting, or character, or deeper thematic threads that fortify a thesis. And it might be that a writer has only one character in his or her essay—a poorly drawn character who needs fleshing out—or perhaps other characters that need to be introduced so that we see many points of view.

I imagine that your job, Dave, when you embark on putting the Adventure Essay together after all the prewriting and the research is done, is one of knowing which kid needs which kind of layering and how much. And then staying on top of the process of layering. Tuning in to the student and his or her essay is the hard work of teaching writing, but it is essential because no two writers need to work on the exact same elements of the craft.

The exciting thing is that when you Dave work with a ten- or an eleven-year-old writer, asking questions like, Is this part here missing anything? or Since your main idea is X don't you think we need to show it with a little more Y?—asking these kinds of technical questions is really about bending the young writer's mind, making him or her reach out for something to layer into their essay to make it a stronger, more believable, and more forceful argument. This is the never-ending task of a writer, to make an endless array of choices. The teacher teaches just by asking effective questions.

Pete's thoughts helped me see writing in a different way, not so much as a flat chronological time line of settings, characters, and events, but more as a three-dimensional web of interconnected elements, each playing a vital role in the composition. I try to help my students understand writing through this lens, as a layering of information and ideas. In writing conferences, I ask students to go back and layer in more details. For example, if a student is writing about volcanoes in Hawaii, and there's little reference to the topography of the islands, I would show him how to layer in more geographic details—not a section of writing pertaining to geography, but rather an awareness of the geography throughout the essay. If a student is writing about a historical figure from Virginia, I might make sure that the historical layer to the whole essay is appropriate and sufficiently supportive to the main idea. Pete's layering approach enables kids to be successful at this idea of blending narrative writing with researched information, because it makes the transitions natural and seamless. It also gives them a real sense that their essays don't have to be perfect the first time round, but rather gain strength over time and in various drafts. In fact, it was this layering idea, more than anything else, that allowed me to make the jump from the stagnant research report to the detailed and vibrant adventure essay.

Making Time for Conferencing

Once the adventure is under way, each writer takes off in his or her own direction. Knowing ahead of time where their paths may take them is helpful to some students, who might otherwise be a bit lost. Of course, oftentimes the kids change their minds along the way and create new paths as their research guides them in new directions. In either case, they move forward in their adventures, writing about their journeys as they progress from one point to another within their respective states. I emphasize that each stopping point in the journey, each new character they meet, and each new bit of information they uncover should ultimately be helpful to them in resolving their story. Keeping them on track and guiding them through the process is essentially our role as teachers. Sometimes the best way to do this is through examples. We often start a writer's workshop with a mini-lesson or by sharing writing samples to emphasize this point. Ultimately, though, the only way to ensure a successful outcome is through individual writing conferences.

In fact, as the essays progress, there is a continual need for more and more writing conferences. The project would not be possible without them. It isn't feasible to meet with every student every day, but checking in with all students and conferencing with a third to a half of them daily is my goal. This is definitely the most challenging time for me as a teacher, because if a few days go by without conferencing with them, I can get so far behind that it's difficult to catch up.

I'm lucky to work with an amazing team of teachers and assistants in our classroom. During this part of the writing process, we often conference with kids simultaneously and are thereby able to meet with all kids more frequently. After class we frequently talk with each other about the progress students are making or the obstacles they're encountering in their writing. There's a great sense of camaraderie and common purpose among us as we work together to find the best ways to guide the students through the challenging steps in this writing process. Before conferencing, we like to know exactly where each kid is in his or her essay and where he or she needs to go next. For this reason, it's helpful to have the kids type their essays into a computer. We can go to their files before class and reread their essays. If there are specific areas that need attention, I save a copy of the essay and insert comments using the track changes feature in Microsoft Word, or I use the highlighter tool to draw attention to these areas. That way I have something to point to during the writing conference, and they have something to refer to after I've left and have begun working with another student.

I like to begin writing conferences by acknowledging the students' progress and verifying that they are on track with their essay. Then I ask them questions about the direction they're heading in, such as, *Where are you going next? Why are you going there? How will this contribute to your quest/thesis? Will you meet a new character there? What new information will you get from this character that will help you in your quest?* I usually offer suggestions. I might ask them to go back and layer in more essential details in one area or cut out erroneous details in another. They may be drifting off topic and need some guidance to become refocused on their goal. I like to end a conference by giving an assignment, maybe to do a bit more research on a subject, or to rethink and recast a character into a new one who might be more helpful to the goal of the essay. Or it might be something as simple as asking them to find a hotel where they plan to stay at the next stop in their adventure. Encouragement at the end is also essential. These basic components help give some much-needed direction and keep kids motivated. All writers need feedback, especially ten-year-old writers.

Although some of the general components of a conference may be similar, the substance is completely different for each kid. Not only are the essay topics different, but the emphasis kids put on a certain subject will vary according to their specific interest in it. In one kid's essay I might be excited to see one or two pertinent details included about a subject, whereas with another kid's essay, I would be surprised if there weren't seven or eight pertinent details attributed to the same subject. Understanding what individuals are capable of writing and making time to conference and guide them in their own direction is what makes this project work for every kid.

Making Modifications

A buzzword these days is *differentiated instruction*, but the term really applies in the adventure project, especially in an inclusion classroom like ours, where there's a tremendous range of abilities and needs. All the kids can write this adventure essay, but they all do it in their own way. Each kid has particular areas that they need help with, and the writing conference is the perfect place to point these areas out and to find ways to improve them. In the end it's these individual goals, efforts, and areas of growth—worked out in conferences—that really shine in the adventure essay.

Here too, I'm lucky to work with a tremendous team of teachers who help make many of the necessary modifications. Since we begin the adventure project later in the year we have a fairly good sense of our students' abilities and areas of need from the start. As we go through the process, we make adjustments and modifications for individual students to ensure that they'll be challenged but not overwhelmed.

For some special needs students, modifications may be something as minor as giving extra one-on-one time during the research portion and conferencing more regularly during the writing portion. Or we might scale back the project a bit and, for example, only require them to visit three locations in their state instead of five in the writing of their adventure. Many times it means helping these students find a quest that will be manageable based on their reading and research abilities. This might mean avoiding obscure topics and searching for ones that will be found more easily in multiple resources. For the students who struggle with reading, we allow the use of a software program called WordQ, which reads the text of Web sites.

For a few students, we've even made modifications to the way in which the adventures were presented. A couple of years ago I had a special needs student who really struggled with writing, but he was great with visuals. Instead of the typed adventure essay, he created a PowerPoint show that included some writing with photos of his state adventure. His story was well told, and he did a wonderful presentation for the class at the completion of the project. Since the project is vast in scope, there are an equally vast number of ways in which to modify it. Finding the right modifications for each special needs student is a process that changes as the project unfolds. We continually discuss the students' needs, figuring out what works and what should be tweaked so that everyone can succeed in it. Brett Adams and I have worked together in this way for so long that we can almost read each other's thoughts. And as this project has evolved over the years, we've worked together to continually improve it.

Step 6: Completing the Project

In the end, each adventure must come to a satisfying conclusion. To help students with this, I have them focus on two basic elements that should be present near the end of the essay: resolution and reflection. When we get to this point in the writing process, we go back and reread the final pages of Pete's *The Lost Treasure of Captain Kidd*, in which he satisfies the reader by answering the last few unresolved questions. The story ends with the main character, Alex, looking back on his adventure and reminiscing about his days of treasure hunting. (See page 147 in Appendix A for a handout that helps students with this portion of the project.)

Resolution

The students need to wrap up any loose ends in their story and resolve unanswered questions. This is sometimes difficult for kids to see in their own writing, because they're so engrossed in their adventures that they can't always look at their own work objectively. I prompt them with questions. *So what ever happened to so and so? How did your character get back home in the end? What happened to the lost diary once it was turned over to the police?* Most kids need a few prompts to help them remember which loose ends are still out there.

Another strategy is to have kids work with a partner to peer edit. Asking them to fully edit the entire essay is asking too much (for fifth graders, at least), but getting them to simply read a peer's essay from beginning to end and jot questions for the writer on a pad of sticky notes is reasonable. Often kids will find little things that I've missed. This process helps not only the writer, but also the reader. When students have to look for unresolved issues in another kid's writing, they quickly realize that they have a few unsolved issues in their own essays. It helps them look at their own writing with a more critical eye.

Reflection

After addressing all of the unresolved issues, I ask my students to end their essays by reflecting on the events of the story. Although not all great adventures necessarily end on a reflective note, I find that encouraging students to do this helps bring closure to their essays. This doesn't have to be a long or complex portion, simply a moment of looking back over the time spent on their journeys. Maybe the closing takes place many years later, and the character is looking back on the time she spent helping the homeless in New Orleans after a hurricane nearly destroyed that city. Or maybe, as in Klara's essay, the journey ends with a research biologist traveling home to New York and thinking back on the events that transpired during her time spent in Alaska.

> It's been wonderful watching the puppies [wolf pups] grow up and I hate to leave . . . On my plane home to Albany I remember the year I spent with the wolves in Alaska. I have learned many things about them that I could never have learned from school or from books. It's been wonderful being in Alaska, home to the last true wilderness in the United States. I hope my research will help people better understand these magnificent animals. As for the dogs, I think they enjoyed this trip as much as I did, and that's definitely saying something. I know that one day I'll return to this land, the kingdom of the wild wolf.

By this point in the process, after many weeks of researching and writing, the kids are ecstatic with the realization that they've completed this monumental task. But another part of them is almost sad to see their adventures come to an end. They've become so connected to their research topic through the writing of these essays that they sometimes want to keep it going.

A great way to keep the stories alive is to celebrate and share them with their classmates. For several days after the essays are complete, we take time out of the day to read the stories aloud. Each day I choose three or four new readers to share their essays. I ask the other kids to sign up for an adventure that they'd like to hear. I try to make sure that each reader has a sizeable audience, but the groups usually work out fairly evenly on their own. Dividing the class into three or four groups makes it more manageable for me, and it allows the readers to have a smaller but more engaged audience.

Last year the weather was nice, and we sat outside for several afternoons reading essays in small groups. The kids absolutely love this! For the reader, it provides a tremendous sense of satisfaction to see that their writing is so engaging to their friends. For the audience it's great to see how their friends' stories have come together in the end. In most cases, whether through class discussions, or peer editing, or conversations, kids know about each other's adventures. This is a time to see the whole piece—together and complete. After each reading, the kids always have questions for the writer and have discussions within their groups. This process of reading the adventure essays aloud and talking about their writing brings a satisfying closure to the project and leaves everyone with a genuine sense of accomplishment.

The Adventure Essay
by Peter Lourie

Dave's Adventure Writing Unit gets kids thinking about this blend of fiction and nonfiction, another reason his approach is so exciting.

And this—Dave's process of connecting student writers to subjects they feel passionate about, his emphasis on setting and character, his requirement that his students do the legwork either in books, from films, or especially from the Internet—is what makes his approach to the research paper so exciting. It requires his students to work both in nonfiction and fiction, sometimes blurring the line between the two, both working toward one common narrative goal.

But the main point here is that Dave's layered approach to the adventure-based research paper gets students thinking about how to bring information and research into the arc of their stories. He shows them examples of writing, both fiction and nonfiction, in which the writers succeed. At the same time he shows them examples from student papers where information is not woven into the text but is, rather, plunked down into the essay as if it were a heavy load of rocks sitting in the middle of a putting green.

At some point in the process, too, the students undergo a vigorous peer review of their essays, and it's almost always the case that fellow students can see what a young writer cannot see in her own essay. Having extra eyes going over papers at various stages in the revision process and commenting on each other's papers with respectful and constructive criticism helps students more seamlessly blend information into their stories.

No one said learning to write would be an easy process. It's more mind- and heart-bending than not. But the students in his class, so invested in their own fictional adventures, approach the research paper not as some dead artifact in the dusty basement of a venerable museum, but as a living thing. They actually go out into the world, albeit sometimes more on the Net than in reality, to draw upon the experience of others and to glean facts, history, information, and details that they then use to fashion and support their own theses. The specifics they have discovered find their way into their papers. The information from the great world out there is used to support their new-found passion for Adventure Writing.

Step Four

Technology

Chapter 8

Technology

Using Technology in the Field
Peter Lourie

Portable audio recorders, digital cameras, high-definition camcorders—these are the tools of my trade. Oh, and notebooks and pens. When I begin an adventure, whether to the Arctic or the Amazon, I bring plenty of tools to record the details of my journeys. Not being blessed with a photographic memory, this is the only way I can come back with the rich layers of material (stories, characters, history, atmospheres, settings) that I need to write my adventure books. What makes these tools so important in the digital age is that I can use the sounds and pictures—and now HD video clips—in ways that are complementary to my writing. Telling the kids about a particular experience in the jungle is nowhere near as dramatic as showing them howlers running through the trees and stopping to roar or whales surfacing and blowing water vapor from their blowholes in the Beaufort Sea. I like to use photos, tape recordings, and videos to excite kids about ancient cultures, distant lands, and foreign places. I also can use short clips on my Web site or blog. (In fact, I developed a whole Web site around such digital stories [http://www.arcticstories.net/]. Iñupiaq Eskimos and scientists alike tell their own stories in their own words, all of which I hope will demystify the Arctic and bring the complex issues that exist above the Arctic Circle into people's homes.) I sometimes sell photos and footage to national magazines. And I always end my writing workshops with stories about collecting material in the field.

But I don't want to give the impression that this is tedious work. In fact, it's a ton of fun. I love holding a camera or tape recorder; I love to capture such rich stories for future use. Since good writing is detailed writing, I show kids how much detail I can collect with these instruments of my trade. When I get back I listen to the tapes and look at the photos and video, and from these records I write my first drafts.

The truth is, if I were a kid today, I might choose to become a videographer rather than a writer, because on video you can collect setting, character, and history all in one dynamic place. Video is so immediate and exciting. With Movie Maker or iMovie or the one I use, Final Cut Pro, a videographer can create rich and exciting adventure stories. For now, however, my collections of digital files are used to write more effectively. They help me remember: DETAILS, DETAILS, DETAILS.

Using Technology in the Writing Classroom
David Somoza

I never intended to use technology to such an extent in the teaching of writing, but it sort of evolved over time. And I keep stumbling on new ways to use various forms of technology in teaching kids to write.

When most teachers think of integrating technology into teaching, the first subject that comes to mind is usually not writing. But when you think about writing as a way of connecting with the world, it makes a lot of sense to use technology to help kids create this link. This is particularly true for a research project like the state adventure, where the Internet can become the vehicle that connects the kids with the world (see Chapters 6 and 7 for a full explanation of the project). Maybe it's just for a brief while to gain a better understanding of another place, another person, or a potential adventure, but the Internet allows kids to have virtual adventures and bring back valuable information. In fact, without the aid of the Internet, the state adventure project could not be developed to the extent that we do, because it's the addition of online research that allows us to better ground the adventure essay with factual and detailed information. It's this detailed information, so easily accessed through online research, that allows us to revive the research paper and turn it into a journey that is deeply personal.

In addition to the Internet, there are many easy-to-use software programs available that can synthesize images, audio, and video to create multimedia vignettes that can launch an adventure project. Once these vignettes are created, the presentation equipment is key to the effective delivery of this material to students. In other words, the kids will become engaged in the video and music to a greater or lesser degree depending on the equipment used to present it. With a larger, clearer image and with higher sound quality, students will become more engaged in the writing prompt—and therefore more engaged in their writing. The combination of equipment, programs, and Internet-based research makes for technology-rich, multisensory experiences for the writing student. Ultimately, it's what takes them out of the classroom and into the world.

Part 1: Creating and Presenting Multimedia Writing Prompts

In Chapter 4, we talk about the need for creating different experiences for the kids. Through multimedia writing prompts we introduce our students to adventures by allowing them to see and experience places that are new and foreign to them. It's this sense of the unfamiliar in these varied "virtual experiences" that make the adventure come alive in their writing. Here are a few ways we've been able to use technology to create these writing prompts. Web sites and tutorials are listed in the "Resources" at the end of this section. For more details on the lessons involving these writing prompts and their connection to the adventure project, refer to Chapter 4.

Images and Music

Something as simple as projecting a landscape image while playing background music can be very effective. When the lights go out in the classroom and an image of a distant land appears on the screen, the kids' imaginations begin to take off. The addition of music heightens this experience and introduces a certain mood or flavor that is otherwise missing. Each visual image of a setting can be paired with its own unique music, which enriches the writer's experience. You might try a few different settings. Initially, I used images of my own: a jungle clearing in the rain forest, a snowy trail along a steep cliff, a view across a parched desert valley. Select images that are obviously of faraway and magical places, ones that will invite exploration.

Before you start, tell your students to begin by clearly describing the setting. Follow this by inviting them to go on an adventure in this new land. It doesn't have to be a full story, just an experience. Afterward, take time to read the writing aloud. You'll be amazed; even with the same multisensory prompt, students have incredibly varied and unique experiences—each a completely fresh take of the new and unfamiliar scene. Over time, the writing will start to have a feeling of awe, and it will seem that the narrator is experiencing this place for the first time.

Video Clips

If you want your students to gain more information about the setting from the visual prompt, you might want to present a video collage with various scenes. Using Windows Movie Maker or Apple's iMovie, you can combine short video clips and layer in background music to develop a much more complex scene as a writing prompt. Windows Movie Maker is a standard feature on most PCs. If you don't have it, check for free downloads online.

Locating video clips is the first task. There are many different places to find videos online, but saving them is not always permitted. An educational video database like Discovery Education Streaming makes this easier. Many school districts subscribe to this service. If yours does not, check on their Web site to see if you can get a thirty-day trial offer. I was able to do this several years ago. Power Media Plus is another free education video source. Once you have a video source, download short clips that relate to the scene that you want to create in the writing prompt (the Amazon rain forest, the Sahara Desert, Maya ruins, etc.).

Open Microsoft Movie Maker and follow the steps to create a new video project. First you will be prompted to import your video clips. Then you'll drag your clips into Movie Maker's storyboard. Now your video clips are loaded into your new Movie Maker video project and you can begin editing them. Maybe you only want the first thirty seconds of a video; you can crop the video clip with Movie Maker editing tools. You probably won't need more than three or four minutes of combined video to create a powerful writing prompt. Once the clips are edited, you can begin working with the audio. Most educational videos have narration, which would be distracting in a writing prompt. Fortunately, the narration can be muted. To the left of the storyboard is the word "Video." Beside it is a blue "+" sign. Click on the "+" sign, and it will change to a "–" sign. This will expand and open the audio track (narration). Right-click on the audio track, and click "mute." Then click on the "–" sign. This will mute the narration that came with your video.

Next you'll need to import your own music. Look for music that will complement, not distract from, the scenes in the videos (I prefer instrumental music so that there are no words to distract the kids as they write). Once you've imported your music, drag it to the "Audio/Music" layer of your storyboard. Design the movie so that the music and video begin at the same time, but when your video clips end, allow the music to keep playing so the video fades to black but the music continues playing for thirty minutes or more. You'll find that a total of three to four minutes of video is plenty and gives students some powerful images in a short amount of time. They can keep writing with only the music playing, making new visuals in their mind's eye. All of the steps in this process may sound complicated now, but as soon as you try it you'll see how intuitive it is.

This synthesis of music and video is amazingly motivating to kids. The sensory input in an otherwise dark space focuses their attention and bombards them with strong impulses to leave the school environment and travel in their minds to these other worlds. Their writing will reflect these rich, new experiences. This is the beginning of the process of connecting writing to the adventure essay that they will be working on later.

Photo Stories

A simpler alternative to this video-making process is to combine still images with music using Microsoft's Photo Story 3 or Soundslides. These programs allow you simply and quickly to import photos and music and combine them to create a movie of your own. You can use your own images or photos found online. TrekEarth has a photo gallery with high-quality photos from all over the world. Using the Ken Burns Effect feature, the still images pan and zoom to create the illusion of movement, an effective presentation that became very well-known through Ken Burns's documentaries. The process is so easy to use that you can create an incredibly powerful multimedia writing prompt in no time at all. Our fifth-grade team now makes video prompts using Photo Story 3 on a regular basis, and we have fun doing it!

Begin by finding photos and music that you want to use for your video prompt. You can download Photo Story 3, from Microsoft, for free onto your computer (I've heard that Soundslides is also a wonderful program, but I haven't used it). Once you've downloaded Photo Story 3, click on "begin a new project." Then import your pictures. You can rearrange your photos to create the sequence you like best. The next step is adding titles (I usually skip this step for writing prompts, because I don't want to put my own words into any student's head). The following step lets you customize the motion of the zooming and panning. Adjust the setting for each photo until you have them the way you like. The next step allows you to add background music (click "select music"). This allows you to browse through your files to find the music you want.

Once you've imported your music, you will be able to see the track highlighted as a bar above the photos on the storyboard. Now you can go back to the "customizing motion" step to adjust the display times of each photo to coincide with the piece of music you've selected. Here, too, three to four minutes of total run time is sufficient. Now you can click on "preview" to see how your video will appear when finished. We usually end up going back and adjusting a few details at this point. When you're satisfied with it, go to the final step and save it. The finished file will run as a video on Windows Media Player or any other media software.

The last step is to import your photo story into Movie Maker as a video. We do this so that we can add additional music, which will continue to play after the video has finished. Once you've imported your photo story into Movie Maker, import more music and drag it into the storyboard beyond the point where the video ends. As I've mentioned, we usually have about thirty minutes of music that continues beyond the video. Save the video and try it out. You'll see that your photo story fades to black and the music keeps going. This is when your students will dive into their writing. I keep the lights dimmed so kids feel like they're still in this other world.

Since we can't easily take our students out into the world, we can bring the world to the students. These little movies do exactly that: bring new places and experiences into the classroom. And it's in this world that students can explore new paths of writing.

Classroom Equipment

So how do you present these multimedia writing prompts? It's wonderful to have a classroom full of great gadgets to enhance the learning experience for the kids, but I taught for many years without them. Creating the right environment for kids to explore writing in a new way can be as simple as turning off the lights and playing the right music, or projecting an image from a slide projector on a whiteboard. Of course, having great audiovisual tools at your disposal makes it even easier to achieve this goal. Over time I've written grants for most of the equipment in my room, and it was well worth the time spent.

Audio

Surround-sound systems, designed to work well in a single room like a living room, work very well in a classroom too. I got a very inexpensive system ($250 on sale) that enhances the sound tremendously. With five speakers mounted around the room, the stereo is crystal clear and equally audible in all parts of the room.

Visual

For years I had a TV, which served as a presentation tool. However, displaying an image on a larger surface allows kids to see the details more clearly and draws them into the writing prompts more effectively. Schools often have a multimedia projector, which can be used to project images onto a large surface. After borrowing one for years, I finally wrote a grant for one of my own last year, and it has made a tremendous difference. With the image displayed on the whiteboard and music playing through the surround-sound system, my students can feel like they are really leaving the school and heading off for an adventure in another part of the world. It's like having a movie theater in your own classroom. If you're using video writing prompts, this is the way to go.

Resources

+ TrekEarth photo gallery: http://www.trekearth.com/gallery/
+ Photo Story 3 can be downloaded for free at:
  http://www.microsoft.com/windowsxp/using/digitalphotography/
  photostory/default.mspx

- ✦ Photo Story 3 Tutorial: http://www.windowsphotostory.com/ Guides/Beginner/importing-and-arranging-pictures.aspx
- ✦ Soundslides Web site: http://soundslides.com/
- ✦ Discovery Education Streaming: http://streaming .discoveryeducation.com/
- ✦ PowerMediaPlus: http://www.powermediaplus.com/
- ✦ Movie Maker can be downloaded, but it is installed on most newer PCs: http://www.microsoft.com/windowsxp/downloads/ updates/moviemaker2.mspx
- ✦ Movie Maker Tutorial: http://www.microsoft.com/windowsxp/ using/moviemaker/getstarted/default.mspx
- ✦ iMovie: http://www.apple.com/ilife/imovie/

Part 2: Using Online Research Tools Effectively

Using the Internet for research with students can be a wonderful experience or a very frustrating one. Mostly, this depends on two things: the level of teacher preparation and the type of preteaching that takes place before the research begins.

Teacher Preparation for Research

Try to imagine exactly what the kids will do during the research process. *What exactly will they be looking for? Where will they look? How will they search? What tools are available to guide them? What will they do with the information once they've found it? How will they record their sources?* Answers to these questions will help in preparating for a large-scale research project.

For fifth graders, I'm usually fairly clear about what I want them to look for in their research. Beginning this way helps ensure that they're successful in their research early on, which builds confidence while they're honing their research skills. Later in the project, there will be many areas that the kids will explore more independently, but I like to begin by guiding them in a clear direction. This content is included in a WebQuest specifically designed for this project. The information is organized by subject within the WebQuest to facilitate the research process.

The part of the WebQuest that is most crucial to the success of the students in their research is the list of Web sites that you provide them. The Internet holds an endless supply of resources, where reliable information is interspersed with unreliable information. Much of their frustration can be minimized if we do some research ahead of time to locate several reliable and effective resources for each section of their research. These resources are integrated into the WebQuest so that the students have what they need at their fingertips. In the end, they'll go off and find many other sources on their own, but these basic reference Web sites will serve as a starting point for all the kids.

When introducing my students to the WebQuest and the Web sites, I like to do a tutorial, a sort of walk-through. Here it's helpful to have a multimedia projector to present the information as the kids follow along on their computers. In addition to showing them the layout of the WebQuest, I like to walk them through the major Web sites that we'll be using to show them how they're organized. Then they'll have time to explore the sites on their own before any of the research begins. These few extra steps will really save time in the end.

Once the research begins, the kids will need a place to record the information. I design the WebQuests, as I think most teachers do, as a template with tables and boxes so that students can take notes right in the WebQuest packet. I used to have them write the information there, but I've found that it's more effective, for fifth graders at least, to have them type the information into the packet. For this reason I've made all of the text boxes and tables with expandable cells so that the kids are not limited in the amount of text that they can add to any one area. Typing rather than writing makes it less likely that kids will lose their work. It's also helpful for the students later, when they're writing their adventure stories, to pull up their research on a minimized screen. They often have their adventure essay open on one half of the screen with their research open on the other half. This allows them to go back and forth, pulling researched information into their essays.

Another great advantage of templates has to do with bibliographies. Since many of the students' resources for the adventure project are online, they'll need to record the exact URL of each Web site. It's easy for fifth graders (for any of us, really) to make a small error when copying extensive Web addresses. So it's much more efficient and accurate if they can copy and paste these URLs directly into a textbox. I like to build simple templates for bibliographic information right into the WebQuest packets. This way as the kids locate their information, they can quickly copy the URL from the Web site and paste it into their document. I encourage them to do this as they go, but I end class by reminding them to add new Web addresses to their list of URLs before saving and shutting down each day. This has been helpful for two reasons. First, it allows the kids to return to the Web sites anytime they need to gather more information. And second, of course, it gives the kids a compiled list of bibliographic information that they'll use in their bibliographies at the end of the project. (See pages 120–134 in Appendix A for an example of the State Adventure WebQuest. The bibliography table is on page 134.)

Preteaching for Research

In addition to teacher preparation for research, there's student preparation. A few simple mini-lessons taught ahead of time can save hours of frustration and make the research process more efficient and enjoyable for kids.

I like to begin by explaining a bit about the Web. We usually have this discussion along with a demonstration on the multimedia projector, so kids can see a search in progress as we discuss the issues. Most kids who have not had much exposure to research believe that everything on the Internet is factual. I like to explain that anyone can contribute anything they'd like to the Internet, so some of it is reliable and some of it is not. My students often think that the first site that pops up in a search list is the best one to use. I explain that the first one in the list is simply the one that other people have opened the most. This doesn't necessarily mean that it's a source that will work best for them. This leads to the point of the first lesson: How do you know the difference between reliable and unreliable resources? I do tell them that many of the Web sites we will use are ones that I've selected for them, but they need to understand that they too can and should be critical of resources and make their own judgments about the reliability of a Web site before quoting it.

So where do you begin? I'm sure that all teachers have their own way of distinguishing between reliable and unreliable Web sites, but a few basics that I usually discuss are Web site suffixes, source, date of publication, and content. Most kids I teach don't know that the Web site suffix can give you information about the source (.com is a company, .gov is a government agency, .edu is an educational organization, etc.). When conducting research, knowing this information often helps steer you toward or away from a source. Sometimes you can also tell a bit about the source by looking at the rest of the Web address. Other times you have to open the Web site and look at the information posted about the source. I also show students how to find the date of publication because in some cases this may be very important. For example, I tell them if you're trying to find the population of a city, you probably want the most recent data available. After going through those steps quickly, we discuss the need to be critical as we read the content of Web sites. This isn't something that kids will be able to do perfectly the first time, but I stress the importance of keeping an open mind and checking facts with multiple resources to verify information before swallowing it hook, line, and sinker. The truth is, the more they learn about a subject, the more discerning they become, simply by virtue of their own level of "expertise."

The next logical lesson, then, might be research ethics. What do you do with the information you find? We talk about the difference between plagiarizing and quoting information from sources. Kids usually understand this quickly if you relate it to fairness. What if I took John's math homework, erased his name, and put my name on it? You get the point. This is a very important lesson because with limited exposure to research most kids simply don't realize that copying something word for word and/or forgetting to cite sources is not acceptable. I like to follow up a discussion like this by showing kids how to paraphrase. It's important to show them that they often only need a small portion of what they will find. Narrowing it down is the first step; reading it and making sense of it is the second step; and rewriting it into something that is useful and understandable is the last step. We practice this skill before research begins.

For students who struggle with decoding, a great preteaching lesson is showing them how to use a program called WordQ during the research process. The program works in tandem with other programs and will read text to students, including the text of any online article. For students who can understand material that is read to them but can't always read it themselves, WordQ is perfect. It allows them to gain the information they need without being inhibited by their disability.

Another great preteaching lesson for all students is to demonstrate some of the little skills that we, as adults, take for granted when we research online. I show my kids how to open a link in a new window or a new tab, how to minimize and maximize documents on the task bar, how to quickly go back several steps in a search, how to mark Web sites as favorites, and how to copy and paste URLs into their WebQuest packets or bibliographies. There are probably many more lessons that can be taught prior to research, but with just these basic ones under their belts, students will be able to conduct their research more effectively and more wisely.

Having some familiarity with the Web and understanding a few basic navigation tools will also assist students as they move through their worldwide adventures. For the state adventure project, the Internet functions as a substitute for the travel experience, so kids need to be able to use it well if they're going to have a memorable journey.

Part 3: Celebrating Student Writing Through Digital Writing Portfolios

Writing plays a major role in our classroom throughout the year, from the first description of a setting to the final draft of the adventure essay, so naturally I want my kids to share it and celebrate in their accomplishments. To help in this area, I've found a very simple tool: the digital writing portfolio.

Throughout the year, as students complete their final typed draft of an essay, they save a digital copy in a special folder on their student server. At the end of the year this special portfolio folder is filled with their best pieces of writing. The students then create a table of contents and a cover page on the computer, which they also save into their portfolio folders.

Using simple hyperlinks (highlight text, right click, and go to "Hyperlink"), kids create links between the items listed in their table of contents and the essays in their portfolio folders. At the end of each essay, I have the kids create links "Back to the table of contents" and onward to the "Next writing sample." Finally, they will create a link between their cover page and their table of contents. When we finish, the kids test their links to see that they all work properly. With all of these linked items in the same folder, it's easy for me to save each kid's portfolio to a CD.

Keeping a hard copy is also nice for the kids, so I have them print final versions of their writing pieces, and we bind them into simple books. Then I attach the CD in a sleeve to the inside cover of the book. The kids take these finished portfolios home on the last day of school as a memory of their writing experiences in fifth grade. I encourage them to save their digital portfolios to their home computer and continue to add to them as they develop new pieces of writing. Several students have come back to tell me that they have done exactly that. My hope is that they'll continue to value writing and that they'll see it as an incredible expression of themselves for years to come.

One thing is for certain, every student who has worked with us on the adventure-based essay has made great strides toward becoming a better writer. What makes this whole project special for me, and I hope for them, is that we all have worked together; we have written to explore our best selves; and we have taken a great adventure—diving into our passions and learning the craft as we journey forth.

Appendix

Handouts and Activities for the Adventure Writing Project

Part

1

Research

State Research:
WebQuest Activity Packet

Name: _____

Process: The research for this project is broken down into three sections. First, you'll search for general information about your state. Second, you'll look for photographs from your state. Third, you'll look for information that deals with several specific areas. The three parts of your research will give you a great foundation for your project, so let's get started.

Writing to Explore: Discovering Adventure in the Research Paper, 3–8 by David Somoza and Peter Lourie. Copyright © 2010. Stenhouse Publishers.

General Information About Your State

Use the following Web sites to find the answers to questions listed on the following pages.

Grolier's America the Beautiful
An excellent source for general information about each state. To access it from home, click on the link http://auth.grolier.com/login/go_login_page.html. Check with your teacher to get the username and login.

Class Brain
Similar to America the Beautiful in that it offers a great deal of general information about your state. http://classbrain.com. Click on "State Reports," near the top.

Netstate
General information about each state in the United States. http://www.netstate.com/states/index.html

State Government Web sites
Links to state Web sites. http://www.kids.gov/k_states.htm

ProTeacher
Lessons and links for each state. This site is designed more for teachers, but you can find some good information here. http://www.proteacher.com/090082.shtml

USA.gov
Government links for each state. Each state is set up differently, but most contain tourist information and photos, and some include videos. http://www.usa.gov/Topics/Graphics_State.shtml

Use the Web sites listed here to answer the following:

A. Geography

1. To which U.S. region does your state belong?

2. Name all bordering states, oceans, or countries:

_____

_____

_____

3. What is the state capital?

_____

4. Name the five largest cities in your state:

_____

_____

_____

5. Are there any national parks or national monuments in your state? Name them:

_____

_____

_____

_____

6. Name all of the major landforms in your state—lakes, rivers, bays, mountains, plateaus, deserts, etc.

_____

_____

_____

_____

_____

7. What is the average elevation above sea level in your state?

_____

8. What is the highest point in your state?
Elevation: _____
Location: _____

Writing to Explore: Discovering Adventure in the Research Paper, 3–8 by David Somoza and Peter Lourie. Copyright © 2010. Stenhouse Publishers.

Writing to Explore: Discovering Adventure in the Research Paper, 3–8 by David Somoza and Peter Lourie. Copyright © 2010. Stenhouse Publishers.

B. State History and Present-Day Culture

1. In which year did your state become part of the United States (statehood)?

_____

2. What is the population of your state?

_____

3. What is the ethnic makeup of your state (use percentages or population figures)?

_____

_____

_____

4. Name the primary immigrant groups that originally settled in your state.

_____

_____

_____

5. Which groups of Native Americans lived or still live in your state today?

_____

_____

_____

6. List the major events in your state's history. Use additional paper if necessary.

Date	Event

7. Name some important people in history who are from your state.

Who are they?	For what are they famous?

8. What are some important cultural events that take place today in your state?

_____

_____

_____

9. Name the most common tourist attractions in your state.

_____

_____

_____

C. Economy

1. What are the major industries of your state?

_____

_____

2. Where are the major economic centers of your state located?

_____

_____

3. List the most important natural resources that come from your state.

_____

_____

D. Foods

1. List the major agricultural (farm) products from your state.

    _____

    _____

    _____

2. What are some common traditional food dishes that come from your state?

    _____

    _____

    _____

3. Later in the spring, we will have a state food day celebration at school. Choose a recipe from your state and write it below. You may decide to change your idea later, but at least you'll have a recipe to fall back on if you need it.

    _____

    _____

    _____

    _____

    _____

    _____

    _____

    _____

    _____

    _____

    _____

    _____

    _____

Photographs from Your State

Use the following Web sites to find the images required for this section.

✦ The TrekEarth Web site has a great set of photographs from each state. To find photos from your state, click "Search" on the left-hand side of the screen. Type in your state name, and click "Go." On the next screen, click on your state name when it appears. There are several pages of photos for each state! Along the left-hand margin, towns and cities from your state will be listed in alphabetical order. You can either click through the photos to find what you want, or you can click on a town name to find a specific photo. http://www.trekearth.com/gallery

✦ Photographer Quang-Tuan Luong has beautiful photos from many of the states. There are two sections you'll find useful—North America, and the U.S. National Parks. http://www.terragalleria.com

✦ The Class Brain Web site has state photographs. Click on "State Reports," then click on your state. Scroll down to "Photos and Media." http://classbrain.com

✦ National Geographic photo gallery. Here you can find information and photos. Use the following Web site, substituting your state name for California in the Web address. http://www3 .nationalgeographic.com/places/states/state_california.html

✦ Links for each state. Each state is set up differently, but most states contain photos, and some include videos. http://www.usa.gov/ Topics/Graphics_State.shtml

✦ Photographs of some of the Western states. http://www.lumika .org/usa.htm

✦ Photographs and links to parks and forests of each state. However, some of these photos cannot be copied. http://www.myparkphotos .com/state-public-properties.html

Writing to Explore: Discovering Adventure in the Research Paper, 3–8 by David Somoza and Peter Lourie. Copyright © 2010. Stenhouse Publishers.

State Photographs

Find at least ten photographs of your state. Try to find interesting places that you would like to learn more about as you get further into your project. You should include at least *five photographs of natural settings* and at least *five photographs of cities, towns, or villages* from your state. Be sure to give each photo a name that will help you to remember it. Fill in the URL (Web address) for each photo in the following table. It's also a good idea to save each photo into a folder on your computer.

Come up with a name for each photograph	URL of photograph

Focused Research

Use the specific Web sites indicated to find answers to each activity or set of activities listed.

A. Transportation

Create a detailed map of your state. To do this, first find a good road map. You can use a paper map or you can find one online. Several of the Web sites listed in the "General Information About Your State" section have state maps.

Print out an outline map of your state. Find and label the following items on your map. Be sure to include a key so that you can later identify all symbols used on the map.

1. Important cities
2. Major airports
3. Train stations and railroad tracks (Amtrak)
4. Interstates and U.S. highways
5. Major rivers and waterways

To print out an outline map, go to the Netstate site, http://www.netstate.com/states/index.html. On the left you'll see a list, click on "State Maps" and find your state. It will give you several map options.

B. Travel Time and Distance

To find directions and travel time between any cities in the United States: http://www.mapquest.com or http://www.googlemaps.com

To find the distance between any two cities as well as the latitude and longitude of each: http://www.indo.com/cgi-bin/dist

Use these Web sites to find out the travel time and distance from your home town to the capital city of your state (by car). Also find the latitude and longitude of your starting and ending points. Record your results in the following table:

Travel Time	Distance
Latitude and Longitude of Your Home Town	**Latitude and Longitude of Your Destination**

Writing to Explore: Discovering Adventure in the Research Paper, 3–8 by David Somoza and Peter Lourie. Copyright © 2010. Stenhouse Publishers.

C. Climate

Several of the Web sites listed in "General Information About Your State" will give you climate information about your state. Use them to fill in the following tables:

1. What are the average temperatures in your state during the winter and summer?

Winter:	Summer:

2. What is the yearly amount of precipitation in your state? What is the yearly amount of snowfall in your state?

    Note: You may only be able to find precipitation, not specifically rainfall or snowfall. In that case, just leave the snowfall blank and fill in the rainfall box with precipitation totals.

Annual Rainfall:	Annual Snowfall:

D. Time Zone

A time zone map gives current time in each state. To find the time zone for each state, go to http://www.time.gov/.

Use this Web site to fill in the following tables:

What time is it now where you live?
What time is it now in the state that you are researching?
What is the approximate time difference in hours?
What time zone is your state in?

E. Local News: State Newspapers

To learn about local news from your state, find a newspaper from a town in your state: http://www.usanewspapers.com/.

Find a newspaper article about something that interests you in your state. Write a brief summary of the article here:

Name of Newspaper:

_____

Town or City of Newspaper:

_____

Title of article:

_____

Date:

_____

Summary of article:

_____

_____

_____

_____

_____

_____

_____

_____

_____

_____

_____

Writing to Explore: Discovering Adventure in the Research Paper, 3–8 by David Somoza and Peter Lourie. Copyright © 2010. Stenhouse Publishers.

F. Places to Visit

As you start to think about your adventure in this state, find at least five places you would like to visit in your state. These may be cities, national parks, historical sites, natural wonders, and so on. Be sure to choose places from various areas around your state. You may use any of the Web sites listed in this WebQuest or in the "General Information About Your State" WebQuest to help you find information about these places. Also use a map of your state to plan your route.

List the five locations here in the order in which you plan to visit them, then fill in specific information for each in the tables that follow:

_____

_____

_____

_____

_____

Place Name	Location	Photograph Name	Photograph URL
Description of the place using information from your research:			

Place Name	Location	Photograph Name	Photograph URL

Description of the place using information from your research:

Place Name	Location	Photograph Name	Photograph URL

Description of the place using information from your research:

Place Name	Location	Photograph Name	Photograph URL

Description of the place using information from your research:

Place Name	Location	Photograph Name	Photograph URL

Description of the place using information from your research:

Bibliographic Information for State Research

Name: _____

Use this bibliography sheet to record basic information about your resources so that you can create a final bibliography at the end of your project.

Resource Name	Bibliographic Information for Each Resource You Used

Part

Adventure Essay

What Makes an Adventure an Adventure?

Elements of an Adventure Story as It Relates to the State Adventure Project

✦ The story is realistic and believable (not fantasy).

✦ The main character (or characters) is looking for something very important.

    ✧ He or she is on a personal quest to find it, but there are problems or obstacles along the way that often include suspense/cliff-hangers and exciting events.

    ✧ These events or episodes often deepen the main character's problem; the goal is harder and harder to reach, until something changes in the story that helps resolve the problem.

    ✧ The storyline is full of twists and turns, often involving risk or personal danger; it keeps the reader interested.

✦ There is a solution to the problem(s) or some type of resolution near the end of the story.

    ✧ The main character is relieved at the end when he/she accomplishes the goal or finds some resolution.

✦ Setting(s):

    ✧ New and unfamiliar places (setting may be dangerous or it can become an obstacle, making the quest more difficult).

    ✧ Usually involves some traveling.

    ✧ Descriptive language is used to help the reader clearly imagine the setting.

✦ Character(s):

    ✧ Although most adventure stories have one main character, they almost always contain more than one character so that the reader can relate to at least one character (for example, in *The Lost Treasure of Captain Kidd*, we can best relate to Alex, but it wouldn't be an adventure without Killian).

    ✧ Characters must be believable.

    ✧ Conversation/dialogue can take place between characters (information can be shared with the reader in this manner).

    ✧ Other characters (who might come from a new and unfamiliar place) can help the main character by sharing key information that will help in his or her quest.

✦ Descriptive language is used to help the reader clearly imagine the characters.
+ History (Background):
✦ Woven seamlessly into the story.
✦ The idea for the quest can be linked to the history of the place.
✦ Folktales, myths, legends, or local stories can be included.

Remember:

+ You will be the main character in your story. In your adventure, you can make yourself older than you actually are, give yourself an occupation, and so forth, to make your story believable.
+ That which you are looking for must also be realistic/believable— something that is unique to your state and something that you could actually find there.
+ Remember that you are, in some ways, blending fiction with non-fiction by creating a character who will be moving through a real world in a real state. This is really the biggest challenge.

As you write your adventure, refer to this list from time to time. It will serve as a good checklist and a means of keeping you on track. As you write, you may also think of other elements of adventure stories that we haven't included. Add these new ideas here:

_____

_____

_____

_____

_____

_____

_____

_____

_____

_____

Adventure Planning
Travel Plans

Name:	State:
Starting Point: **Season:**	
Means of Transportation:	
What are you searching for?	
Why is this important to you?	

Event(s): What will happen here?	Location
First	
Second	
Third	
Fourth	
Fifth	

Now, write about why you will be going on to the next location. What leads you from one location to the next? How will you get to the next location?

Transition	What leads you on?	How will you get there?
From first location to second location:		
From second location to third location:		
From third location to fourth location:		
From fourth location to fifth location:		
From fifth location to home:		

Adventure Writing Project: Putting It All Together

Setting the Scene

Name: _____

Choose a photo of a location in your state where you would like to begin your adventure. As you study your photo, imagine that you are in it—that you are standing inside of that scene. On the lines below, describe your surroundings.

You may start with a general sentence that tells the reader where you are, but don't include the name of your location or state yet. For example, *I'm over-looking an enormous, rocky canyon.* Follow this up with careful descriptions using rich vocabulary to explain details of what you see, feel, hear, and smell. You may include descriptions that include the season, the weather, the land-forms, the colors of the sky, the smells of the plants, the sounds that could be heard there, and so on. Try to use similes and/or metaphors to make your writing richer. You may also want to use words like foreground and background to guide the reader's eye to certain areas of the photo. End your description with feelings or thoughts that you have about being in this setting.

The reader should be able to clearly imagine the scene and feel that he/she is there also.

_____

_____

_____

_____

_____

_____

_____

_____

_____

_____

(continue on loose-leaf paper)

Student Sample 1

Lost in the Tundra
by Kylie

I am in a kayak in the Bering Sea. The large shadows of the mountains in the distance stand tall, as I watch the sun slowly set. My kayak shakes and the water starts to make a circle of ripples. I look down into the murky waters and hear a large wail. The tiny boat starts to shake furiously as I look around in panic. Suddenly, a giant Bowhead whale breaches and sends me into the dark depths of the sea. I struggle to get to the surface but the unbeatable waves pull me deeper and deeper until everything goes black.

Student Sample 2

My Very Own Mystery
by Jack

As I walk down the street of this colossal city, I can't help but notice what's around me. When I look to the left I see stores, street vendors, and people of all sorts. As I look to the right, I see cars and buses rushing by. I hear the honking of horns, the hollering of pedestrians, and just regular city life. As I look up, I see towering buildings (at least 150 feet tall) that seem to be attached to the cloudless blue sky! They have so many stories and windows, you couldn't even imagine.

Right as I turn off of Roosevelt, and onto Lake Side Drive, my breath is taken away at this fantastic sight. I see the Field Museum approaching out of the distance, standing side-by-side with an early morning sunrise. Right then I think, "I have to go there."

Writing to Explore: Discovering Adventure in the Research Paper, 3–8 by David Somoza and Peter Lourie. Copyright © 2010. Stenhouse Publishers.

Getting There

Name: _____

In this portion of your adventure, you will describe in detail how you got to the location that you wrote about in the "Setting the Scene" section of your adventure essay.

You may start with a general sentence that tells the reader how long it took you to get to this place and where you came from. For example, *It had taken me nearly three days of travel to get here from Albany*. Follow this up with careful descriptions using rich vocabulary to explain details of your travels. You may include descriptions that include the means of transportation used to get here, the places you briefly stopped along the way, any difficulties you encountered along the way, and so on. You should include names of towns, highway numbers, names of airports, train stations, rental car agencies, and so forth. (*Note: Google maps may be helpful in planning for this part of your adventure.*) End with a description of how you feel to finally be here.

The reader should be able to clearly imagine what all you have gone through to get here.

_____

_____

_____

_____

_____

_____

_____

_____

_____

_____

_____

_____

_____

_____

(continue on loose-leaf paper)

The Quest

Name: _____

In this portion of your adventure, you will describe in detail what you came to find here and why it's so important to you.

You may start with a general sentence that tells the reader what you have come to find and when your desire to search for this thing began. For example, *For the past seven years I had been researching Ponce de Leon and his explorations through Florida.* Follow this up with careful descriptions using rich vocabulary to explain the importance of your search. For example, *Now, I'm heading to Florida to meet with fellow historians, study original artifacts from his journeys, and follow the paths that he took. In doing so, I hope to learn more about this early American explorer and come to know what his life may have been like as he journeyed through this beautiful land.* You may include descriptions that include the ways and places in which you researched this topic or searched for an artifact in the past. You may also give a few clues as to what you believe you will find in this location or along your journey. This is where you have to really hook the reader and get him or her excited to read on. End with a description of how you feel to finally be here in this spot and about to begin your quest.

The reader should be able to clearly imagine what all you have gone through to get here and should share your excitement about your quest.

_____

_____

_____

_____

_____

_____

_____

_____

_____

(continue on loose-leaf paper)

Writing to Explore: Discovering Adventure in the Research Paper, 3–8 by David Somoza and Peter Lourie. Copyright © 2010. Stenhouse Publishers.

What a Character

Name: _____

In this portion of your adventure, you will describe in detail an interesting character who you meet in your adventure. This character should help you to solve a piece of the puzzle in your quest. This can be an imaginary character or a real one from your state.

You may start with a general sentence that gives the reader a sense of the setting where you plan to meet this character. For example, *There, in the back of the library between rows of tattered books stacked high, sat the old geezer.* Follow this up with careful descriptions using rich vocabulary to make the character come alive for the reader. For example, *His rumpled beige corduroy jacket and narrow spectacles gave the impression of a scholarly professor from years gone by. As he turned I saw in his eyes a madness, a fever, an undying desire to find this treasure, even if it meant putting his own life in danger.* You should include both physical descriptions as well as descriptions of your character's personality. In addition, you may choose to include dialogue, which will help bring out the character's personality. In the dialogue be sure to include such things as the character's mannerisms, accent, and word choice to help define this character. End by showing the reader how this character will help you in your quest.

The reader should be able to clearly imagine this new character you've just created.

_____

_____

_____

_____

_____

_____

_____

_____

_____

_____

(continue on loose-leaf paper)

The Adventure Begins

Name: _____

Now that you are in your state and we know what you're here to find, you will take off and search for it. This will be the longest and most exciting part of your adventure. This is the section where you will include your researched information about your state.

You may start with a sentence that lets the reader know that your quest has begun. For example, *I woke up early that morning, because I was anxious to get going.* Follow this up with careful descriptions using rich vocabulary to explain how and where you search. As your adventure unfolds, be sure to describe places that you come upon and people whom you meet. Also include your thoughts and feelings along the way. Remember to stick to the subject—be sure that the places that you visit and the people whom you meet are helping you to get closer to the object of your search. Along the way you will come upon obstacles, but be sure that you get back on track once you've overcome each obstacle. Be sure not to end it too quickly or too easily—draw the reader into your story. End this section with a wonderful description of how you actually find the object of your search. At the end of this section your problem must be solved.

The reader should be able to clearly imagine what all you are going through as your adventure unfolds.

_____

_____

_____

_____

_____

_____

_____

_____

_____

(continue on loose-leaf paper)

Writing to Explore: Discovering Adventure in the Research Paper, 3–8 by David Somoza and Peter Lourie. Copyright © 2010. Stenhouse Publishers.

Resolution and Reflection

Name: _____

By now you have already completed your search and found the "treasure" that you've gone looking for. In this final section you need to complete two important things. First, you have to end your story in a way that ties up all of the loose ends and satisfies the reader. Second, you need to reflect or look back on your adventure and remember the highlights.

You may begin to plan for this section by going through your story and finding any "loose ends" or unanswered questions. Then you have to come up with a creative conclusion in which you answer these questions and leave the reader with a feeling of satisfaction. In the second half of this section, you should look back on your adventure and remind the reader about the story and how it unfolded. You may also want to include in this section new things that you learned as a result of your trip, or you may want to show how you've been changed by this adventure.

Peter Lourie shows us a great example of this in the final chapter of *The Lost Treasure of Captain Kidd*. First, he resolves the unanswered questions through the letter from Killian to Alex. Then he reflects back on the whole adventure and shows how it has changed him. Before you begin writing this section, reread this chapter from Peter Lourie's book.

_____

_____

_____

_____

_____

_____

_____

_____

_____

_____

_____

(continue on loose-leaf paper)

Appendix

Student Writing Samples

State Adventure Essays

The finished adventure essays tend to be lengthy, but not all are as extensive as the examples shown here. I chose Katie and Klara's essays because they are so complete. They were both so taken by the project that they put in many extra hours finding details from their research and weaving them into fairly sophisticated story lines, especially when you consider that they're only fifth graders.

Our primary goal with this project was to give our students the understanding that comes with creating an imaginative, well-crafted, and research-based adventure essay—an experience in which their writing is guided by their research, and their research is guided by their writing. These two essays exemplify this process in every way.

Benjamin Franklin's Lost Invention

by Katie

Fisher Fine Arts Library, University of Pennsylvania, Philadelphia.

The cold spring air sends a shiver down my spine as I walk nearer and nearer to the clay-colored building. It's not the color of clay people dye when they make it into shapes, but the color it is when it's dug out of the ground. Small, detailed designs cover the huge building. Green grass around the bottom, and a brick pathway leading up to it, make it look like a palace. The bright blue sky in the background owns not a cloud. Flowers bring a sweet smell to the fresh spring air. Bare trees almost have leaves on them. My back is warmed by the sun, which is now high in the sky. It's hard to imagine that this great university has been traced back to 1740, only 59 years after Pennsylvania became a chartered territory! The people here must have done a lot of rebuilding over time. As I walk up the many steps to the door, I can't help but say to myself, "I can't believe I'm actually here!"

That "I can't believe I'm actually here" moment took awhile to finally arrive, and so did I. I awoke at 7:00 a.m., made sure I had everything, and then headed out the door. Putting all my bags in my car took longer than I had expected, because I didn't want all my belongings falling on me while I was driving to the train station. Though I had arrived at the Amtrak station in Schenectady later than I had planned, I still had enough time to get ready and board the 9:20 train. My train stopped at Penn Station in New York City, and after about 45 minutes, we boarded again, but this time to go to 30th Street Station in Philadelphia. I wanted to get a little rest on the train, or at least just have a peaceful, quiet ride. That didn't happen, though. It's not exactly a "peaceful" train ride when the large man next to you has music blaring, then falls asleep and snores extremely loud.

I walk up to the check-in desk at a bed-and-breakfast called The Columns on Clinton, after arriving in a taxi. The Columns on Clinton, being built from 1854–1856, was meant to be a federal town house. It was then expanded in 1878, and remodeled in 2000. My room feels nice and cozy, with a mahogany bed, a warm floral comforter and a mahogany dresser. Plus I have a coffee maker, coffee, and all sorts of creamers, and that means I won't have to buy any . . . YAY! I will definitely enjoy staying in this room, as well as this state. After settling in, I take another taxi to the restaurant I had looked up on the computer at home. It's called Liberties Restaurant and Bar. Trying to decide what to get to eat is the hardest thing ever, but I finally decide on the Philly Cheese Steak, which sounds extremely delicious! Boy was I right!!! When you hear "Philly Cheese Steak", your mouth starts watering, right? Well, wait until you actually taste it! Liberties is a tremendous family-friendly place to eat, with families laughing, talking, and cracking jokes everywhere you look. It is about 7:00 p.m. when I get back to the bed-and-breakfast. Knowing I have a long day ahead of me, I get all set for bed, and I read my book until around 9:45, when I fall asleep.

For the past three years I've been researching Benjamin Franklin and his inventions. I heard a story about him from my friend Julia, who I met in college, and immediately became interested. Nearly a year later, Governor Edward G. Rendell asked me to find it: the lost invention of Benjamin Franklin. I guess Governor Rendell chose me for the job because I'm a detective, and a rather well known one at that. This is one of the most exciting jobs I've been asked to do so far! A diary supposedly was taken about one year ago from a house Franklin once lived in. No one knows who took it, or why, but the state thinks the individual is undercover somewhere in southeast Pennsylvania. It was reported to the state police that a man with blond hair, glasses, and dark blue eyes was seen with an object that looked like an extremely old-looking diary, or notebook, jump into a black Ford Focus with a Minnesota license plate that read BLM~3549. I was thinking about how many people have black cars, blue eyes, all the characteristics he has, and plus license plates are sometimes very difficult to read. For all I know, that may not even be him! This is a one-of-a-kind mission, and the state is counting on me, and so is Benjamin Franklin. It won't be easy, but I'm determined to find this diary!

It is 9:00 when my alarm goes off, and I crawl out of bed to take a shower. I am lucky, considering the University of Pennsylvania is only eight minutes away. Wanting to be as prepared as possible, I grab my notebook and a pencil and my purse with extra pencils and pens, water, a few snacks, money, my guidebook, and a small map. Catching a taxi is exceptionally easy this morning, since it is a Sunday and nobody has to go to work; well, except for me, of course. The ride is a rather difficult one, taking into account that there are three car crashes along the way, and the main road is blocked. We have to take a different route, which takes much longer than planned.

The upside is that the landscape is pleasant to look at. Streets are lined with trees that are starting to bud. I can feel the fresh spring air, and I'm relaxed, even though I arrive nearly 30 minutes later than I had anticipated. It takes awhile for me to locate the library, but after asking several of the students, I finally find my way. My heels click as I walk across the floor. I spot an elderly woman with white curled hair putting books on the shelves, and try to grab her attention. "Excuse me?" I say.

"Why hello young lady," she answered. "What can I do for you?" She is wearing dark brown pants and a flowered button-up blouse.

"Where could I find some information on Benjamin Franklin?"

"Well you're looking right at it! In fact, I was his next-door neighbor!" She lets out a little laugh, and so do I.

"Now you know I'm just kidding, sweetie." I am beginning to like her. "My name is Rosemary Cairo. I'm the librarian here."

"I'm Killay, Katie Killay."

"Getting back to your question, I have a few books here, but not much. I do, though, have a friend who knows oodles about him! Actually I haven't seen Jon in forever." She walks over to a huge bookcase that has "HISTORY" written across it in big bold letters. Rosemary quickly grabs a few books and hands them to me. "I hope this helps," she tells me. "You should stay here to look over them. Classes will be over soon, and you don't want to get run over by billions of college students, now do you?"

"Thank you so much!" I say as I settle myself and crack open a book. The books only give me information like "Benjamin Franklin was born in 1706," or "Ben Franklin was the 15th of a candle maker's 17 children." There is another book on Pennsylvania's history, so I decide to take a look at

Writing to Explore: Discovering Adventure in the Research Paper, 3–8 by David Somoza and Peter Lourie. Copyright © 2010. Stenhouse Publishers.

it. "In 1701 Philadelphia was incorporated as a city. Then, only about 5,400 people lived there. Then by 1720, it had grown to around 10,000 people." That's interesting, I think. "By the middle of the 1700s, it was one of the leading cities in the colonies." This is fascinating information, but I have to get going. Except for the Pennsylvania book, all this was information I already know, so I decided to ask Rosemary for the address of this man named Jon she had been talking about.

As I walk up she says, "Did they help?"

"Not much," I reply. "Can I have the address of that man you were talking about? The one who knows a lot about Benjamin Franklin?"

"Sure, sweetie." Rosemary takes a sticky note from the front desk and quickly scribbles something on it.

"Here. 500 Chestnut Street, Independence Hall. Ask for Jon Bachus. He should be there."

"Thank you so much!"

"Any time, dear. Tell me how it goes. If you need anything, you know where to find me!"

"OK. Bye Rosemary. Thanks again!"

"Goodbye Katie."

I really hope that Jon can help me. I decide to take a horse and carriage to get to Independence Hall. The horse is a dark coffee brown and her name is, well, Coffee. Finally after nearly 10 minutes, we turn left onto Chestnut Street and we're there. It's an average 60 degree spring day. Thankfully all the snow is melted, so it is rather nice out. Independence Hall is a big brick building with glass windows and an arched doorway. People are walking everywhere, and cars are driving around the cobblestone road. The driver stops the carriage and I hand him a couple dollars.

After I get out, I have to push through the crowd. The front desk is right inside the door. There is a chubby man sitting there with his feet up on the desk, and, even though he is missing a few teeth, I decide I should still ask him about Jon Bachus.

"Whadaya want?" he says.

"Is there a Jon Bachus here?"

"Naw." He goes back to reading the newspaper. Well that was rude. Right near the desk there's a big sign, so I walk over to it. It says, "Independence Hall was built between 1732 and 1753. The constitution was written here in 1787. It was very hot that summer, but the windows had to be kept closed, so no one would hear the conversations. This building is sometimes called the birthplace of the United States of America. The last time it was restored was in 1950, so it would look like it did in 1776."

Writing to Explore: Discovering Adventure in the Research Paper, 3–8 by David Somoza and Peter Lourie. Copyright © 2010. Stenhouse Publishers.

A minute later I walk back over to him and say, "Do you know where I can find him?"

"Yah."

"Where?" Nothing. I'm getting really frustrated at this point. "Excuse me sir, where can I find—"

"I told ya, he's not here!"

"Where can I find him?"

"Ugh. Would ya stop botherin' me?"

"Sir, I need to find Jon Bachus." I repeat.

"Go ask someone else."

I walk away, tremendously frustrated with him. There's a woman at another desk on the second story. She has a nametag on that has "Theresa" written on it.

"Excuse me?"

"How may I help you?"

"Is there a . . . a Jon Bachus here?"

"Sorry, but he passed five months ago." Now what am I going to do? Go back to Rosemary and tell her he was dead? I guess maybe I shouldn't.

"Does he have family around here?"

"He has some family in Amish Country in Lancaster. He was once Amish, too, ya know."

"Where'd he live?"

"Little village called Bird-in-Hand."

"Okay. I'll try it. His name?"

"Frank Himmel. Good luck with whatever you're here for."

"Lost diary of Benjamin Franklin." She immediately jumps up.

"WHAT? Are you crazy???"

"Maybe I am." I let out a little laugh.

"No, no! You can't! You can't do that!"

"Why not?"

"Do you know who has it?"

"Um . . . no but I think I know what he looks like."

"What do ya think he looks like?"

"It's right here in my notebook." I open to the first page. "Let's see. Blond hair, glasses, blue eyes. That's all I have."

"Almost 5 feet 10 inches?"

"I don't know! I gave ya all I got."

"Well, what you got so far sounds just like . . . just like . . . oh, never mind."

"Just like who?"

Writing to Explore: Discovering Adventure in the Research Paper, 3–8 by David Somoza and Peter Lourie. Copyright © 2010. Stenhouse Publishers.

"I can't tell you. I'm sorry."

"Why? Do you know them?" The woman looks shocked.

"No!"

"Why can't you tell me!?!"

"Because I can't. Anyway, it's time for my lunch break. Goodbye," she says as she darts away. Well that was rude. Now how would I find Frank Himmel? Maybe there would be some sort of community event going on. What kinds of things would the Amish do as a community at this time of year? Easter is a few weeks ago. Christmas is long gone. What else do they celebrate around now? What do they do as a community to help one another? I will have to do some more research, but that will have to wait until tomorrow.

A taxi finally stops for me and I climb in and tell the driver where I need to go. I am looking over my information, thinking about the day, and that woman at Independence Hall, Theresa, when all of the sudden I hear a loud noise and am leaning toward the other side of the taxi.

"What was that?"

"Well, I believe it's dat tire 'gan."

"You've got to be kidding me," I mutter.

"I ain't."

"Now what?"

"We wait."

"For . . .?"

"Another taxi, a tow truck, I don't know. Whatever comes 'long."

"Couldn't we call someone?"

"No. They won't care."

"Well, I need to get back to my hotel pronto. How far is Clinton Street?"

"I don't know. I jus' drive 'round." He has a heavy southern accent.

"Well, I sort of need to know to get back there."

"That's somethin' you got to figure out on your own cuz I don't know." I take my purse and jacket and step out of the taxi. It looks like I'll be walking, since there isn't another taxi in sight. High heels are not good shoes for walking on the side of the road, trying to figure out where you are. My feet are sore, my legs are sore, and I don't know exactly where I am. Plus I am tired. I'm not about to thumb a lift, because this is a big city, and it would be too dangerous. It is around 6:00 p.m., so most of the stores are closing, because it is a Sunday. Good thing the sun is still out, giving off plenty of light, otherwise I'd be in the dark.

I walk for a while then realize not many people are out here. Now, not only am I wet, tired, and a little chilly, but I am lonely, too! I guess everyone

Writing to Explore: Discovering Adventure in the Research Paper, 3–8 by David Somoza and Peter Lourie. Copyright © 2010. Stenhouse Publishers.

is inside eating dinner. This had not been a good day. Some people are so difficult to deal with, like the man at Independence Hall, and others just like to get on your nerves, like that woman Theresa! And now, to add to it, I am sort of lost. I don't want to admit it, but I have to. All I want to do is go back to the hotel, get in my pajamas, and sleep. Just sleep. Sleep for as long as I can, without anybody bothering me. Maybe I'm not the right person for this assignment after all. I feel like I've failed. I've failed Governor Rendell, I've failed the state, I've failed Benjamin Franklin, but most of all, I've failed myself.

There is a park up ahead, so I decide to go in and sit down. As I walk in, I notice the name. Independence Park. Wait. That has to be near Independence Hall, doesn't it? Great. I'm right back where I started. My life is getting worse by the minute. This could be good though, couldn't it? Shouldn't there be police or something on night duty? I think I might be in luck. First, though, I have to find my way back to Independence Hall. Can I see okay? It's right there in front of me! Well, at least the side entrance is. That is where I went in earlier today. How will I get in to ask someone? Now I have to use the skill that got me into detective work. My creative thinking. If I were a guard, where would I be?

Just then I heard a car drive up behind me. By now it is getting dark. Thank goodness it's a police car, because I am a little nervous. The car stops, and a man rolls the window down.

"May I ask what you ah doing, Miss?" the man says, in a Boston accent.

"Trying to find my way back to my hotel," I reply.

"Why ah you out heah?"

"My cab got a flat tire, so I was kicked out of it, and now I don't know where I am."

"Whe-ah you headed?"

"The Columns on Clinton bed and breakfast. Clinton Street."

"That's a wicked nice place, huh?"

"Yeah. Good service."

"Wouldja like a ride?"

"Please! I would love one!" I let out a sigh of relief.

"You can hop right in the front heah."

"Thanks." It seemed things like this only happened in stories, the real lucky stuff. It only took about five minutes before we pulled up in front of the bed and breakfast. "Thank you so much!"

"Just doin' my job, Miss."

"You can call me Killay. Katie Killay."

"Detective Kill-ay?"

"That's me!"

"Officah Mah-in. Nice to meet you."

"Thanks again, Officer Martin!"

"Have a good night. Stay safe now!"

"I will." I step into the bed and breakfast, take out my key, go down the hall, to room 3. The first thing I do when I get in is take a shower. I am disgusting and smelly. After that, I quickly pull on my pajamas, and hop into my warm, dry, and cozy bed. I don't care that it is only 8:00. All I want to do is sleep.

My eyes slowly draw open around 9:00 a.m. I had slept for 13 hours. I lay in bed, thinking about the day before. Something Amish, something they do as a community. I had to do some research. Before I do anything, I need some coffee—dark with a dash of sweetener.

After I turn on the coffee maker, I pull out my laptop. I take a sip. Okay, now I'm ready. In the search bar I type in "Amish community activity." I click on the first result it gives me. The only thing it talks about is their lifestyle: the clothes they wear, what they eat, and their religion. The second one is more helpful. It says that the Amish have barn raisings in the spring. It's springtime right now! Next I have to find an information center. I type in "Amish information center Lancaster." The first thing to pop up was the Amish Information Center. 2209 Millstream Road Lancaster, PA, was the address. How would I get there though? It says it would be about one hour 30 minutes from here to there, but I didn't really want to take a taxi or a bus for that long. That's when I remember Rosemary. She said if I needed anything, to come to her, and she was only 10 minutes away. I could take a taxi or bus to the University, and then from there maybe Rosemary could drive me.

Today I think I'll take a bus, instead of a taxi. Just for something different, I guess. I finish getting ready to leave, grab what I need and leave. I take the 10:30 bus to the University. "Rosemary? Are you here?" I say as I walk into the library.

"Katie? Is that you?" I hear from behind a bookcase.

"Yah. Where are you?"

"Hold on. I'll be right out." She walks out from behind a bookcase. "How are you?" she asks, even though it's only been a day.

"I'm great. I was just wondering if you could give me a ride to Lancaster."

"That's more than an hour away, isn't it?"

"About one hour and 30 minutes."

"Okay. I'll call a sub in. I'll be right back." Rosemary goes to her desk,

Writing to Explore: Discovering Adventure in the Research Paper, 3–8 by David Somoza and Peter Lourie. Copyright © 2010. Stenhouse Publishers.

and quickly dials a phone number. After a minute or two, she says, "We're all set. She should be here in about five minutes, but we can leave now."

"Okay. Let's go. Here's the address." I say as I hand her the sticky-note.

"Good thing I have my GPS in the car. Follow me." We walk out the door, and straight ahead is an old station wagon. It takes a minute, but it finally starts up, and we're on our way. Rosemary and I are talking about my information in the car.

"Why do you think that woman at Independence Hall was so frantic?" I had told Rosemary about her earlier in the ride.

"Oh, she's known to be like that whenever someone mentions Benjamin Franklin, but no one knows why."

"That's bizarre. How long has she been working there?"

"Two or three weeks, maybe."

"Oh, okay." After that we are quiet for awhile. I am busy staring at the beautiful countryside. The rolling hills are soothing, and look like they were used for farmland. Rosemary says by July, the hills will be filled with row after row of lush green corn stalks. I think about returning then. I'm sure it's even more beautiful.

About a while, Rosemary says, "What are you going to Amish country for?"

"I was told that a man who knows a lot about Ben Franklin is Amish. I wonder if he knows who has the diary."

"Yes. That would be nice."

"That would help me so much. He probably doesn't though."

"You never know," she says.

"Well, it looks like we're here. Thanks again. Sorry for the trouble. Bye." I step out of the car and wave as she drives off. When I walk inside the brick building, I see a woman wearing a solid-colored dress, purple, with a white apron over it, and a white bonnet.

"How may I help you?" the woman says.

"I was wondering if you know when the next barn raising in Lancaster is."

She opens a book, flips a couple of pages, and then says, "Well, it looks like there is one tomorrow afternoon. It's for the Bauer family." The woman has a soft voice. "On 418 Wetherburn Drive."

"Are there any nice hotels or inns I could stay at tonight?" She hands me a list. The first one on it is the Amish View Inn. "How is this one?" I ask.

"It's nice. Not too expensive either."

"Thank you for all the help."

"You're welcome. I'll probably be at that barn raising you were talking about. Most everyone in the community is."

"Great. Thanks! Bye."

"Goodbye," she says. I make a quick call on my cell phone to make sure they have a room for me tonight. They do, so now I just need to get there. Maybe I can relax and take a little break for the rest of the day. I don't see any taxis around here, and I don't think there are any at all in any case. Buggies are everywhere I look. Maybe I could get one of those. It's worth the shot. I walk a little way when I see one of the drivers giving his horse some water.

"Excuse me, sir."

"Why, hello."

"Do you know how I can get to the Amish View Inn?"

"Well I guess in a minute I can give ya a ride. Lemme jus' finish givin' Ol' Murray a drink."

"Okay. Thanks." I look around at the crocuses beginning to pop up through the dark dirt. Beyond the garden area are silos in the distance. Clothes lines are strung across yards from house to barn, the simple clothing of the Amish drying in the spring sun.

"All set," the man says.

He helps me step into the back of the buggy. It is an incredibly cool cart. There are benches on the sides, four windows that are open, and a seat up in front for the driver. On the outside it is black, and "Murray" the horse is dark gray, almost black. Outside the buggy, Amish boys and girls are playing, men and women riding in other buggies and carts, and people scootering down their long driveways to get their mail. When we arrive at the inn and I give the man five dollars, he says, "Na' na', don' need it." He tries to shove it back into my hands. "Keep it."

"No. You stopped what you were doin' so you could help me. I insist. Thank you so much! Goodbye!"

"Bye." I walk into the inn, and immediately notice the intricate pattern of the carpet. The base is dark blue, with creamy yellow swirls and curls. There are sand-colored chairs and dark-brown wood coffee tables. A newspaper and a dark green plant are on each of the coffee tables. The front desk is the same color as the tables, with paintings hanging on the wall behind it. A woman is sitting behind it taking phone calls. I walk up to her, and she says "Thank you" into the phone, then hangs up. "How may I help you?" she asks. She has dark brown hair that goes down to the middle of her back.

"I called about 30 minutes ago, for the Studio Suite."

"Last name?" Her nametag says "Karen" on it.

"Killay. K-i-l-l-a-y."

"Ah, yes. Katie Killay. Second floor, room 32. Here's the key." She hands me a plastic card with my room number on it. "Have a nice stay."

Writing to Explore: Discovering Adventure in the Research Paper, 3–8 by David Somoza and Peter Lourie. Copyright © 2010. Stenhouse Publishers.

Writing to Explore: Discovering Adventure in the Research Paper, 3–8 by David Somoza and Peter Lourie. Copyright © 2010. Stenhouse Publishers.

"Thanks." I pick up my suitcase and walk over to the elevator. Another man comes in. I push the two. He pushes the three.

"What room?" he asks me.

"Studio."

"Deluxe King." The door opens and I step out. When I step inside my room, I am shocked. It is huge. There is a hot tub, a flat-screen TV, a king-sized bed, and so much more. I wasn't expecting something this huge. Well, at least I can relax, just like I had wanted. I set my bag down on the floor and flop onto the bed. It's extremely soft. The rest of the day is spent in the hot tub, and in my bed.

I flip my eyes open around 8:00 a.m. The sun peeks through the window. Around 11:30, I will have to leave to go to the barn raising. That way, I can get there about 10 minutes before it starts. After three more hours of relaxing, I start to get ready to leave. When I'm ready, it's 11:27. Good. I will be just on time.

I get to the house at 11:53 a.m. There are already some people here, so maybe I can ask around to see if anyone related to Jon Bachus is here. I walk up to the first person I see. "Excuse me."

"Hello."

"Are you related to a Jon Bachus?"

"Naw. Sorry lil' miss."

"It's okay." I move on to the next person, who gives me the same response. So does everyone else who's already here. A few more people come, so I ask them, too. The first couple of people don't know him, but when I ask the third person, his eyes light up. "Jon Bachus! Why he was my Uncle. Uncle Jon." The man looks like he is in his mid-eighties. He doesn't have any hair on his head, but his beard definitely makes up for that! It goes three-quarters of the way down his chest. I have never seen a beard so long in all my life! (With the exception of Santa Claus!!!) "So why do you want to know?"

"I'm looking for the lost invention of Benjamin Franklin, and I was told relatives of his would know a lot about Franklin, just like he did."

"Boy is that true! I'll betcha I know more about him than Ol' Uncle Jon did!"

"Can you tell me about him? Ya know, like about how people found his diaries and other important information so I can find the diary with the lost invention?"

"Why not? Would you like to come back to my house? I got my horse n' cart right here. I can't help much with these here barn raisin's anyway. I'm gettin' too old."

"That would be great. Thank you!"

"Would you mind helpin' me walk to the cart?"

"Of course not."

"It's this way. All I really need is someone to help me stay standing." After I help him to the cart and into the driver's seat, he tells me I can get in the back. His house is only 10 minutes away. This man is really good with horses! The guy who drove me to the Amish View Inn and Suites was really good, but this guy is way better. His horse, Idalie, does everything he tells her to do perfectly the first time. When we get back to his house, his wife makes us some tea. "So what did you want to ask me?"

"I have a few questions. The first one is: Have one of Ben Franklin's diaries ever been stolen before?"

"Uh . . . well in fact one of them was stolen three years ago. The man waited two months before he turned himself in. Didn't know what to do wit' it."

"Okay." I write down a few notes about what he said. "Do you know what his name was?"

"Miles Baggly. Got outta jail 'bout four years 'go."

"Do the police know where he is now?"

"They think that he's somewhere around here. He keeps moving around though. Mostly toward Gettysburg."

"Do they know why?"

"No. Maybe he's going to the Abe Lincoln meeting and celebration in Gettysburg National Military Park."

"Okay. What does he look like?"

"Lemme think. I'm old ya know. Can't remember things like I used to. I can only remember a little of it. Blue eyes, blond hair, glasses. His height was in there somewhere, but I can't remember what it was."

"5.10?" I ask.

"Oh, yes. I believe that's it. Any more questions?"

"I was just wondering if you know anything else about Franklin. Like, maybe something that I might find helpful?"

"Ahhh, yes. Did you know that he taught himself to read French, Spanish, Latin, and Italian? That probably won't help you, but I think it's pretty cool."

"Wow. That is cool!"

"Hmmmmm . . ."

"Well, I think that's it. Thank you so much. What was your name again?"

"Frank Himmel. And you are Katie Killay . . . detective." We both broke out in giggles.

Writing to Explore: Discovering Adventure in the Research Paper, 3–8 by David Somoza and Peter Lourie. Copyright © 2010. Stenhouse Publishers.

Writing to Explore: Discovering Adventure in the Research Paper, 3–8 by David Somoza and Peter Lourie. Copyright © 2010. Stenhouse Publishers.

"That's just how I say it! Thank you so much, Frank! I can never thank you enough."

"Don't mention it. I'm glad I can help."

I stand up to leave.

"Goodbye. Thanks again."

"Bye. Good luck!" Frank and his wife wave as I walk down the pathway. Now I have to catch a train to Gettysburg. Miles probably changed his name, and is probably the one who stole the diary. Frank's description is an exact match of mine. I want to leave for Gettysburg tomorrow, because that's the day of the Abe Lincoln meeting/celebration. Another Amish man takes me back to my hotel, and there I buy a train ticket online. My train will leave at 10:30 in the morning, and should get there by 11:15–11:45. It should take about 45 minutes to possibly an hour.

As I fall asleep, I think about the big day ahead of me. This could be it. The day I might finally find Ben Franklin's lost diary.

I wake up at 9:45, pack my bags, and check out. The closest Amtrak station is 15 minutes away, so I arrive there around 10:15. I have plenty of time to board the 10:30 train, so I won't have to worry. Before I know it, they're saying that train 26 passengers have 10 minutes to board. I quickly grab my bags, and get on the train.

I'm so distracted I hardly notice the landscape at first. But when I allow myself to take a deep breath and relax a little, I realize once again how beautiful it is in this state. The lush green trees whip by my window. The yellow flowers of forsythia bushes are striking alongside vibrant red tulips. Spring is amazing.

It is a little late to the station, so I get to Gettysburg around 11:45 a.m. Last night I found a motel to stay in, since I will, in all probability, only stay one or two nights. After I get to the Super 8 motel and put all my bags in my room, I start toward Gettysburg National Military Park. I get there at 12:30 in the afternoon. The celebration started at noon, so most people already are here. I describe Miles to a few people but no one has seen him. Then, I see a man with blond hair, who is a little taller than me. I'm 5.6. He looks *exactly* like Miles Baggly. Now I have to figure out a way to trick him into telling me if he has the diary or not. I walk up to him and start a casual conversation, informing him that I am a history buff and hinting that I am quite wealthy.

"Are you a collector?" he asks.

"Completely," I reply. "And I'll pay top dollar for the right items. I have a particular interest in Colonial artifacts. But they're so rare these days," I sigh.

His eyes light up. "What if I told you," he lowers his voice to a whisper, "that I have in my possession Ben Franklin's lost diary. Would you be interested?"

"I'd have to see it first and validate that it's authentic. How about we arrange a meeting soon? Then I'll need your name."

"Actually, I have the diary with me right now," He pats the bag he has slung around his shoulder, "And the name's Christopher Dunn." Now this was his fake name.

"So, how much you askin' for?"

"Five hundred thousand dollars," he says proudly.

I pause and then reply, "If it's authentic, I'll have the funds wired to you today. Before we proceed, though, let me make sure my bank can wire that much money." That's when I walk away to find the police.

After I tell two officers who I am, I inform them about my conversation with Miles. We sneak through the crowd. They're just about on Miles, and then he sees them. He tries to make a break for it, but they are already too close. They grab him and hand me the diary.

"Make sure this gets to Governor Rendell, and completely undamaged. Don't let anyone see you! Run!" As I sprint through the crowd, I hear Miles yell, "You better be wary, lady. I'll find you!" I stop.

"Really Miles? I don't think so!"

Two weeks later . . .

Today I got a letter in the mail from Rosemary.

> Dear Katie,
> How are you? Did you find the diary and the invention? I hope so. So I guess you caught the person who stole the diary. Miles Baggly, right? It said in the newspaper he was arrested for stealing Ben Franklin's diary. I trust that all is well. We should meet up again sometime.
> Love, your friend,
> Rosemary Cairo

And another from Governor Rendell:

> Detective Killay,
> I owe you my gratitude for finding that diary. It is an important part of our history. Please come to Harrisburg on June 25 to receive your reward. Thank you again. See you soon.
> Governor George E. Rendell

Writing to Explore: Discovering Adventure in the Research Paper, 3–8 by David Somoza and Peter Lourie. Copyright © 2010. Stenhouse Publishers.

On June 25, I go to Harrisburg to receive my reward. When I get to the ceremony, Governor Rendell is there to greet me. "Hello, Detective Killay."

"Hi."

"The ceremony starts in five minutes."

"Okay thanks. By the way, did we find out why that woman Theresa was acting so weird. Didn't I tell you about her?"

"Oh yes. It seems she is Miles' sister, who was going to split the money with him when he sold it."

"No wonder she wouldn't say anything. Thanks." Then Governor Rendell started the ceremony.

"Ladies and gentlemen. Two weeks ago, Detective Katie Killay from Ballston Spa, New York, solved a mystery. A mystery that was important to our state. Benjamin Franklin's diary was stolen on May 26th 2007. We tried many different detectives for the job, but all were unsuccessful. The state called on Miss Killay, and after only a week, so cracked the nut. Though the diary did not include the invention as some had thought, it still is important, and we are very grateful that Detective Killay found it. And now, I would like to call Miss Killay up here to say a few words. Let's give her a big hand!"

I walk up to the stage.

"This was such an important case to Pennsylvania, and to so many people. I'm honored to have been asked to solve this case, and I'm elated to have been able to solve it. I would like to thank everyone who helped me. From Rosemary Cairo, to Officer Martin, thank you all!" I step down from the stage. Governor Rendell says a few more things, and then calls me back up.

"Detective Katie Killay, I would like to present you with these rewards: 500,000 dollars and a plaque under the diary in the Franklin Court." He held up a shiny gold plaque that read, "Dedicated to Detective Katie Killay, who found this diary."

"Thank you so much, Katie."

"Thank you. Thank you, everyone."

This had been the best mystery ever, and I got to solve it. I can't stay still because I'm so happy, even four weeks after.

Katie's Bibliography

Amtrak - Reservations - Fare Finder. 23 Apr. 2009
    <http://tickets.amtrak.com/>.
Bali, Indonesia: Bali Hotels, Tours, Discount and More. 23 Apr. 2009
    <http://www.indo.com/>.

Census Finder - Free Census Records Online. 23 Apr. 2009 <http://www.censusfinder.com/>.

Census Finder - Free Census Records Online. 23 Apr. 2009 <http://www.censusfinder.com/>.

Lancaster County PA Hotel - Amish View Inn - Lancaster County, PA. 23 Apr. 2009 <http://www.amishviewinn.com>.

"Maps." Google. 23 Apr. 2009 <http://google.com/maps>.

The official US time. 23 Apr. 2009 <http://www.time.gov/>.

Penn: University of Pennsylvania. 23 Apr. 2009 <http://www.upenn.edu>.

Pennadutch. 23 Apr. 2009 <http://www.horseshoe.cc>.

Pennsylvania, Pennsylvania Intro, Pennsylvania USA, Pennsylvania Introduction. 23 Apr. 2009 <http://www.pennsylvaniadiary.us/>.

"Pennsylvania." 23 Apr. 2009 <http://go.grolier.com/>.

"Pennsylvania." 23 Apr. 2009 <http://netstate.com/>.

"Pennsylvania." 23 Apr. 2009 <http://www.governor.state.pa.us>.

Pet Names. 23 Apr. 2009 <http://www.funpetnames.com>.

The Sentinel Online: Front Page. 23 Apr. 2009 <http://www.cumberlink.com/>.

Welcome to About.com. 23 Apr. 2009 <http://about.com/>.

Find Bed and Breakfast Inns and Book Online. Over 7,000 B&B's for vacation travel. Unique lodging alternatives to hotels. Buy Gift Cards and Certificates! 24 Apr. 2009 <http://bedandbreakfast.com>.

The Lancaster County Information Center - the Pennsylvania Dutch Country of Lancaster County, PA. 24 Apr. 2009 <http://www.padutch.com/>.

Mennonite Information Center. 24 Apr. 2009 <http://www.mennoniteinfoctr.com/>.

Restaurant.com - Deals on neighborhood restaurants. $25 Restaurant Certificates for only $10! 24 Apr. 2009 <http://www.restaurant.com>.

Writing to Explore: Discovering Adventure in the Research Paper, 3–8 by David Somoza and Peter Lourie. Copyright © 2010. Stenhouse Publishers.

Year of the Wolf

by Klara

Juneau, Alaska

The engine of the jet I am in hums as we fly over Juneau. I look down into the inky waters of the harbor and see a large cruise ship heading towards the city. Juneau is the capitol city of Alaska but it is a very modest-sized city. It looks to me like the entire population of Juneau could squeeze onto the cruise ship heading towards the harbor. Surrounding the city is a thick forest of pine trees, making Juneau look like an island of civilization in an endless sea of wilderness. And that is pretty much what Juneau is.

Goooo! Goooo! wa, wa, WAAAAA! WAAAAAA! Oh, great! That baby sitting across from me is crying *again*! Boy, I'll be glad when this seemingly endless trip is over!

I am so glad to be finally walking through the Juneau international airport. It had taken me seven hours and forty minutes to get here, but it feels like more because I went through four time zones. A furry head brushes my hand. I looked down to see Corva looking right back up at me. Corva is one of my eleven sled dogs that will pull my dogsled while I am here. The rest of my dogs are Aurora, Aquilla, Windy, Marble, Nova, Blizzard, Squall, Hurricane, Night and Titan. All of the dogs are strong and incredibly smart.

Squall, Hurricane, Night and Titan are the only male dogs on my sled team. The rest are girls. Aurora is the lead dog. She is three years old and is a border collie wolf mix. She looks very much like a wolf because of her grizzled grey coat. Right after Aurora on the traces are Aquilla and Windy. Aquilla is a three year old black and white purebred border collie. Windy is a three year old border collie lab mix. She looks like a powerful black lab with white down her belly and white paws with black spots on them. Behind Aquilla and Windy are Marble and Nova. Marble is a three and a half year old blue merle border collie. Blue merle means that Marble's looks a bit like grey marble. Nova is a tri-colored three year old border collie. She is black and white and has tan on her paws and cheeks. After them are Blizzard and Corva. Blizzard is a three year old Samoyed and has pure white fur. Corva is a three and a half year old brown and white malamute/husky cross. Behind Corva and Blizzard are Squall and Hurricane. Squall is Blizzard's litter mate and is almost identical to his sister. Hurricane is a two and a half year old grey and white husky. I got him only a few hours ago in Seattle because my dog team was one dog short. Behind them are the two final dogs, Night and Titan. Night is a powerful three year old black Newfoundland and Titan is a three year old grey and white Alaskan malamute. All of my dogs are behind me right now pulling all their crates, the dog sled and my baggage on wheeled carts.

To get here, I had to go to the Albany International Airport to get on an American Airlines flight that was leaving at 6:20 am in the morning. I arrived at Chicago at 7:40 in the morning. Then I had to wait 50 minutes until my next flight left. During that time I was able to go down to the baggage area and check on the dogs, who were doing well but looked a bit bored. Then it was time to board my next plane which was also an American Airlines. By now it was about 8:35 am. From there I flew to Seattle. I arrived there at about 11:00 am. My next flight was leaving at about 1:20 pm, so I had a few hours to wait. In that space of time, I was actually able to buy Hurricane from a local pound who I had contacted earlier. Then it was on to Juneau on Alaskan Airlines. Finally, I arrived at Juneau at 2:50 pm. To make a long story short, I had a very busy day.

Wow! I am just so glad to finally be here. (So are the dogs, of course). I am sitting in my room at the Juneau Airport Travel Lodge Hotel. The dogs are very happy to be in open space again because I got permission from the hotel manager to allow them out of their crates. I am thinking about all of the amazing things I'll be doing this year. I'll be spending one year traveling around Alaska getting to know several different wolf packs! My aim is to prove to everyone that wolves are not the vicious creatures that they know from storybooks, but in fact, compassionate, respectful and intelligent creatures. If there's anywhere I can find an abundance of wolves—it's Alaska. My field research will concentrate on wolf behavior and the relationship dynamics between wolves in a pack. National Geographic has agreed to fund my research and will publish my findings in their magazine. This is like a dream come true for me because I've been a wolf lover since I was a fourth grader. I have spent four years in college studying animal psychology. Now I will be able to share my love of wolves with the public! I feel like I'm in heaven already!

The next day I decided to take the dogs out for a walk in the city. As we walked about the streets, I realized that I had forgotten something. Maps! I am going to need lots of maps of Alaska! Fortunately, there was a store down the street that seemed to be selling nothing but maps. I bought several maps of the state and an atlas of Alaska. As I flipped through it, I realized that it had more than just maps. It had facts and data tables about Alaska! According to the book, the population of Juneau is 30,711 people. That makes it the second largest city in the state. The largest city in the state is Anchorage. It has 260,283 people. The third largest city in Alaska is Fairbanks. 30,224 people live in that city. Outside, I feel a bit cold and zip my jacket. Even though it's June, the temperature is about 50 degrees. The forest that surrounds the city is made mostly of Sitka spruce trees. The forest stretches for miles and is very rainy, making it the largest temperate rainforest in the world. Tomorrow, I will be going to Prince of Wales Island. The temperate rainforest that exists here also stretches down there. I will be going to the northern end of the island, where there are misty mountains covered in trees. It's a great place for wolves to live. At around ten in the morning, I decided to walk down to the harbor with the dogs. There, I saw an anchored ferry boat. There I saw someone talking to an old man. The person sounded like they needed directions. For some reason the person who was talking seemed very familiar. Then I realized why. It was Jacob! Then he turned around and saw me.

"Hi", he said.

"Hi", I replied. "What are you doing in Alaska?" I asked.

"I'm looking for a rare plant called botrichium plant."

"Oh, cool," I replied. "I'm researching wolves." Then he told me that he had to board the ferry. "Bye", I said as he boarded the boat. Wow, I thought as I walked back to my hotel. Of all the people that I thought I'd meet in Alaska!

The next day, I had to wake up at four thirty in the morning (so did the dogs) so we could go back to the airport. We had a flight leaving at 6:20 that would take us south to Ketchikan National Airport. From there I would take a ferry boat to Prince of Wales Island. On the plane, it wasn't the uncomfortable seats that annoyed me. What really bothered me that sitting across from me, once again, was a baby! Sure enough, I had to put up with cooing and crying for the rest of the flight.

When I got to the Ketchikan airport, I went over in my mind what I was going to do. First I would pick up my rental van. Then the dogs and I are going to catch the 10:45 ferry that would take me to the town of Holis on Prince of Wales Island. We'd arrive there at 1:45. Then we would spend the night in a small log cabin. In the morning we would set off north to the town of Whale Pass. After picking up some provisions, we would set up camp in the forest nearby.

The next day, I got my stuff and the dogs in the rental van and set off for Whale Pass. It was a fairly long trip. All we could see from the car was forest and the occasional pond or lake. The sky was overcast and it rained most of the time. The further north we got, the more mountainous it became. Aurora passed the time by sitting in the front seat and howling. Fortunately, no one else joined her. Finally, we arrived at Whale Pass. It was a small town and, once again, it was surrounded by forest. We made a quick stop at the local food store and then we were off. We drove down a winding dirt road that was surrounded by misty mountains covered in (what else?) dense forest. I heard a noise that sounded like a cross between a growl, a yawn and a whine. (Windy was in the front seat this time, and once in a while she makes that strange noise that I call a "growl-yawn.") When we arrived at a U-shaped valley, I decided that it would be a good place to set up camp. When I let the dogs out of the car, they ran around gleefully, leaving tracks in the dirt road. But then I noticed some fresh canine tracks that I'm sure didn't belong to the dogs. There was only one other animal they could belong to. They were wolf tracks! And there were five sets of them! Wow, I sure did choose the right place to stop! I picked up my bags and set off into the valley, thinking happily to myself that every step I took led me deeper into wolf country.

The next morning, I awoke to the sound of howling wolves. I can't believe I found them so fast! I can't wait to catch my first glimpse of them, but the only way I'll see them today is if they come to me. Wolves are very territorial animals. Each pack, or group of wolves has its own territory, just like people, except wolf territories are much, much larger. Wolves eat, sleep, hunt, play and breed on their territories. Sometimes, neighboring packs may compete over territory, but that is rare. It happens most often when times are tough and wolves need larger hunting grounds. But, when times are good, wolf packs tend to leave each other alone. One thing that wolves can't stand

Writing to Explore: Discovering Adventure in the Research Paper, 3–8 by David Somoza and Peter Lourie. Copyright © 2010. Stenhouse Publishers.

in their territory are other wolves that don't belong to the pack. The wolves would probably see the dogs as intruders and would drive them off. That's why I'm making a barbed wire fence around the campsite today. When I'm out watching the wolves, I'll keep the dogs there for their protection. When I know the wolves aren't nearby, I can let the dogs out. That's why I'm not going out to see them today. But I'll be here for a few months, and I'll have lots of chances to get acquainted with the wolves.

The next morning, I woke well rested and more excited than I had ever felt before. Today, with some luck, I will get my first glimpse of the pack! The wolves here are Alexander Archipelago wolves, a subspecies of the gray wolf. Their scientific name is canis lupus ligoni. These wolves live on many of the islands of the Alaskan panhandle. After closing the gate of the fence I made yesterday, I set out to find the wolves. As I wandered down the valley, I kept my ears pricked for any sound that might help me locate the wolves, such as a howl or a yip, but no sound came. When I reached the valley floor, I saw a large pond with many cattails growing on its banks. There were several fresh wolf tracks in the mud. Then I heard the sound I was listening for. The howl of a wolf. It sounded like it was coming further down the valley. Every shadow looked like a wolf to me now. Then my heart suddenly gives a giant leap. Two amber eyes peer out at me from the brush before disappearing into the depths of the forest. Now is the time for me to be careful. I don't want to make myself seem like a threat to the wolves. So I stood where I was, hoping that he would return but I didn't even see a flash of silver grey fur. Still, seeing a wolf on my first day out was very amazing.

Over the next few days, I kept getting glimpses like I did on my first day out. But I never got a long look at the wolves yet. But my luck was going to change. On my fifth day out, I went to the pond to see if any wolves were there. No wolves, but a piece of driftwood floating in the pond. Then . . . SPLASH! A grey wolf with startling icy blue eyes leapt into the pond and retrieved the drift wood and ran out into the forest.

Fortunately, I was able to tail him, but I made sure that I stayed far enough back that I wouldn't be a disturbance to him. I followed him to an outcropping of rock. There was the rest of the wolf pack. He wasn't the only wolf with blue eyes. There was one other wolf whose eyes were an icy blue. This is very unusual among wolves because even though wolves are born with blue eyes, they usually turn an amber color as the wolf matures. There were seven wolves, and all of them were grey in color except for one that had black fur. I could see that two of the wolves were getting much more respect than the other wolves, who got down low and licked their muzzles whenever they approached them. Those two wolves held their tails high and their ears were pricked, unlike the other wolves, who held their ears and tails low. They were certainly the alpha pair, the leaders of the pack. There are two alphas, one male and one female. They are the only wolves in the pack to have pups. Wolves have a special hierarchy in their packs. The alphas lead, while the others follow and show them respect. Second in charge is the beta wolf. I had a hunch which one that one was. The black wolf seemed to receive a fair amount of respect from its pack mates but it showed great respect to the pair which I was sure were the alphas. Below the beta wolf are the subordinates, a few other adults that live in the pack. The subordinates are constantly trying to become the most dominate subordinate. The lowest wolf in the pack is called the omega. Omegas are often bullied around by the rest of the pack but aren't harmed. The pups are separate from the pack until they are two years old but they have a social structure among themselves that is very similar to what the adults have.

And speaking of puppies, there are puppies here! Five puppies with yellowish brown fur walk up among the adults and begin romping around on the outcrop playing. The wolf that I saw earlier still has the drift wood in its mouth. When a puppy walks up to him he drops the driftwood and the pup immediately starts playing with it like a dog does with its toys. What a fun thing to watch!

Now I know where to find the wolves. More often than not, they are hanging around the outcrop with the pups. I discovered that the puppies' den was very close to the outcrop. Packs with puppies have a meeting place near the den where the wolf pack spends time with each other and the pups. These meeting places are called rendezvous sites. But the one thing I haven't yet witnessed the pack doing is what they need to do to survive—hunt. I have seen them at a carcass, but I've never seen them in pursuit of their prey. In about a week's time my luck was going to change. Around evening, the leader began a chorus of howls to gather the rest of the pack. Then I got very excited. I may finally be able to see a hunt. Down by the pond, three Sitka black-tailed deer foraged innocently by the shore. On the other side, the beta wolf that I am sure is a female stood on a patch of grass, watching the deer intently.

I saw one of the wolves sneak around to the other side of the pond. Then the beta wolf began the chase. It dashed around the pond towards the deer, which fled for their lives. One of the deer looked like it had seen better days. It looked old and it wasn't running properly. As it ran forward, the blue-eyed alpha female sprang out of nowhere and began biting at the deer's legs. The old deer stumbled and fell. It had no escape. The wolves were all around it now and it was dead in a few minutes from loss of blood. The pack had earned their meal, and I had earned a memory that I would never forget.

Writing to Explore: Discovering Adventure in the Research Paper, 3–8 by David Somoza and Peter Lourie. Copyright © 2010. Stenhouse Publishers.

The wolves were very interesting to watch feeding. At meals, the hierarchy of the pack becomes very important. The alpha pair always feed first, then the beta, then the subordinates and finally the omega. Once they had eaten their fill, they all returned to the rendezvous site. There, the pups began to beg for food. They began licking the muzzles of the adult wolves. Then, the blue-eyed wolf that had retrieved the driftwood so long ago opened its mouth and out came the wolf equivalent of baby food—partially digested meat. The pups eagerly began to eat it.

Time sure has flown by. Now it's September and it's almost time for me to leave. I have many memories of this pack. One of my favorites was when one of the puppies leapt high enough to snatch a low flying bird out of the air. I will also remember when the adults all played together and the omega pretended to be an alpha and the alphas pretended to be omegas. I'm sure the dogs will remember this too as they had many chances to explore the forest. I hope I'll be back here someday, but for now I'm setting my sights on Denali National Park.

Today is a very busy day. I have to get back in the van and drive back to Hollis. From there I take the ferry to Ketchikan, where I'll return my rental car. The ferry leaves at 8 am and arrives at 11 am. Then I have to fly to Fairbanks. My flight leaves at 5:22 pm and arrives at 12:51 am tomorrow. Then I'll spend the remainder of the night in a hotel.

Wow! After all of that travel I really don't feel like doing any more. Last night has left me so tired. But I still have one more leg of the journey to complete before I arrive in Denali. Now I'm driving south on interstate A3. Then I have to turn on to Park Road and that will take me into Denali. Finally I arrive in the park. It looks very chilly outside. It's now September 8th and the temperature is beginning to plummet. The forest here isn't as dense and there are some open areas. In one of these meadows I spot a herd of caribou grazing. The mountains here are very tall and steep and some of the taller ones are snowcapped. These mountains belong to the Alaska Range. In this range is the highest mountain in North America: Mt. McKinley. I have to drop the dogs off at the kennel because they have to be leashed in the park and it would be just about impossible to walk eleven dogs at once. The kennel is located in the park near the ranger station and it seems like a dog friendly place. As soon as we get a good enough snow cover, I'll be able to get the dogs out of the kennel and I'll be able to put them on the dog sled. Then I set out for Ruth Glacier in the southern part of the park. When I finally arrived at my destination, it was much less mountainous. I am renting a cabin for my stay here. It is on the edge of the woods next to a meadow created by the glacier. I'm too tired to look for the wolves now; I think I'm going to get some sleep.

The next day, I felt rested enough to go search for the wolves. The scientific name of the wolves here is *canis lupus pambasileus*, another subspecies of the gray wolf. The air outside is chill; my guess is that it is about 40 degrees. The sky is partly cloudy. There are many hills but there are no mountains here. As the day goes on, I find no trace of wolves. Ah, well, you can't always be lucky. Unfortunately, I didn't even get a glimpse of a wolf for about a week, even though I heard them howling. Wolves are incredibly elusive and I'll just have to be patient. My bad luck wasn't going to last forever though. One week after I arrived, I saw a wolf dash across the meadow and catch a snowshoe hare. What an exciting first encounter! The rabbit's fur was nearly pure white but was now stained with blood. The wolf who caught it, who had a grey coat, trotted back to the forest with its prize in its mouth. Quietly, I decided to follow him. He led me deeper and deeper into the forest. In the forest, he was met by a larger wolf whose fur was slightly darker. The other wolf held his tail low and dropped the hare at the larger wolf's feet. Then the larger wolf picked up the hare and ran off into the forest too fast for me to keep up. That wasn't the last of the wolves I'd see that day. In the evening I saw three grey wolves dash across the meadow and into the forest. One of them I recognized as the wolf that caught the snowshoe hare. Over the next few weeks I had similar encounters. I now knew that there were six adults in the pack and three pups. As time progressed, the weather began to get colder. Often I'd wake up to find a light dusting of snow on the ground. It was now early October and the high temperature usually was around 31 degrees with the low being 13 degrees. When we got our first substantial snowfall, I decided to get the dogs out of the kennel. Now they'd be able to do their favorite thing—pulling dog sleds. The dogs went crazy when I picked them up at the kennel. Night was so happy that he knocked me right over! Once we got back to my cabin, they got even more excited when they saw me getting out the dogsled. With the dogsled I will have a better chance of seeing the wolves because I can cover a much wider range than I can on foot. One sunny day in late November I saw another important part of wolf behavior: scent marking. The alpha male uses urine (ha, ha, ha . . .) to mark the trees on the border of his territory, showing other wolves where his territory begins. As I watched him, well, doing his business, he was joined by the two subordinates, both of whose coats were abnormally white. They became very interested in sniffing one of the trees. One of them even stood up on its hind legs to sniff one of the branches.

It's too high up to be a scent mark and I have no idea what they were sniffing. Oh, well. I can't find out everything.

Writing to Explore: Discovering Adventure in the Research Paper, 3–8 by David Somoza and Peter Lourie. Copyright © 2010. Stenhouse Publishers.

It was about nine o'clock the next morning when I got all the dogs hitched up to the sled and head out to the forest. The dogs were going very fast. In no time we were at the edge of the forest, where there were wolf tracks in the snow. We went in deeper and deeper. When we got about a quarter of a mile in, I noticed that there were more and more wolf tracks. Then my heart gave a giant leap. Three wolves were standing in a clearing. From a safe distance I watched them with my binoculars. Two of them showed a lot of dominance over the third wolf, who showed them great respect. Then one of the wolves threw up its head and howled. Soon the forest was full of a whole chorus of howls. The entire pack assembled in the clearing. Then the two wolves that I was sure were the dominant pair set out into the forest with the rest of the pack behind them, with the exception of one that stayed behind with the pups. The alpha female was in the lead.

I followed them by dog sled. When the pack reached another meadow, I spotted a cow moose standing by the edge of the forest. The pack must have spotted her too because they gave chase. As the wolves reached speeds of up to 40 mph, the dogs were having a difficult time keeping up. The moose put on a final burst of speed and the wolf pack gave up. Only one out of ten wolf hunts are successful. I suppose they are just going to have to try again later.

By now it's mid-November. The days are becoming shorter and shorter until one day the sun stops rising altogether. I have seen the pack play together and have witnessed the pups try their luck with snowshoe hares but I haven't witnessed any other hunts. I have seen them at a kill, so they are having some success. Maybe I haven't witnessed many other hunts because dog sled is no longer that reliable, at least not for now because we're having a warm snap. One day, with the dogs back at the cabin, I went to a nearby creek and saw a wolf howling.

I recognized it as the beta male. Soon, the entire pack arrived at the stream. As the pups began to play, one by one the adults joined them. Soon the entire pack was playing tug-o-war, playing tag or wrestling. How fun to watch!

Within a few days, the weather was back to normal with the highs being around 17 degrees and the lows being around 9. We also got several inches of snow, meaning that I could use the dogsled again.

On Thanksgiving, my only table guests were the dogs, who all ate large portions of caribou and turkey. Outside, the wolves' thanksgiving dinner consisted mainly of snowshoe hares. It's pretty far from the lavish dinners back home, but I enjoyed it anyway.

By December, things were really getting cold. The high temperature was 10 degrees and the low was minus 6 degrees. On December 8th, the park was hit by a really bad storm. For a day or two there were blizzard conditions. The weather kept me from the wolves for several days. Finally, one night the storm cleared and I saw one amazing aurora. Unlike many of the auroras I've seen while I've been here, this one is mostly blue instead of green and red. This happens because this particular aurora is lower in the atmosphere than most. It's very fun to watch.

One morning in mid-December, I saw one of the pups attempting to get a snowshoe hare. It was creeping up on it much like a cat does with a mouse. I thought that he probably wasn't going to catch anything; but I was wrong. Once he thought he was close enough he leapt out and caught the rabbit neatly in his teeth. When his siblings came to him, he shared his catch with them.

By now it's late December and I know I'll have to leave soon. I've seen the wolves playing many times, along with howling and trying to catch small prey. But I still haven't witness the killing of a large prey animal. But on Christmas Day, the wolves gave me a Christmas present. In the morning, I saw the alpha pair beginning a chorus of howls in their clearing. Soon the whole pack had gathered there. Then all of the wolves set out for the meadow except for one that stayed behind with the pups. It was going exactly like it had when they tried to get the moose. They were even going back to the meadow. But this time it wasn't moose they were hunting. This time it was caribou. Three caribou are wandering through the meadow. They looked like they had gotten lost. Then I noticed that one caribou had an injured leg. I suspected that that was the one the wolves would go after. Just like I saw with the Prince of Wales Island pack, one of the wolves snuck around into the woods opposite the other wolves. Then the alpha male began the chase. Once again I thought they were going around forty mph. The caribou fled for their lives. The wolves chased them directly towards the forest. Once they had reached the woods, the wolf that snuck around, the beta male, lunged out and began to harass the injured caribou. The other wolves continued to harass the injured animal until it stumbled and fell. The caribou was doomed. The wolves were all around it now and it had no chance of escape. It was dead in a few minutes from blood loss and shock. Wolves help to keep the populations of their prey strong because they prey on the young, old, sick, weak and injured because they are much easier prey. Without wolves, their prey populations would become too large and sickly.

I can't believe how fast these few months have gone. It's already time for me to leave. I will remember this pack and hopefully someday I'll be able to return. But for now, I must move on to my final destination: Gates of the Arctic National Park.

Writing to Explore: Discovering Adventure in the Research Paper, 3–8 by David Somoza and Peter Lourie. Copyright © 2010. Stenhouse Publishers.

Writing to Explore: Discovering Adventure in the Research Paper, 3–8 by David Somoza and Peter Lourie. Copyright © 2010. Stenhouse Publishers.

Oh, no! Now I have to do more traveling! About 400 miles total! And all by car! And in the middle of this permanent dusk! Oh, no! It took about four hours of driving to get to Fairbanks, and another four hours to get to my destination. As I drove I thought about the wolves that I'd be seeing there. The wolves in the park are a mix of *canis lupus pambasileus* and *canis lupus tundrarum*. The wolves in the park usually have light colored coats. In the park, the wolf's main prey is caribou, but the wolves there also prey on moose and Dall sheep. There are no roads in the park, but at one point the highway comes within five miles of the park.

When I finally got to that point, I parked the car near the road and stepped outside to unload the car. Brrrr! It's so cold outside! Here, the average high temperature is minus 4 degrees, and the average low is a bone chilling minus 20 degrees. And that's not even counting the wind chill! Cold or not, I was able to load up my sled and get the dogs hitched up to the sled in the new harnesses I gave them for Christmas. From there, we traveled into the park. The lower part of the park is covered in boreal forest. The Brooks mountain range travels through the park and on the other side of it are vast stretches of tundra. I'd be staying in a rental cabin in the lower part of the park. You need a research permit to do research in the park and fortunately, I was able to get one. It was a long ways to get to the cabin, which was on the edge of the meadow. By the time we got there, even the dogs were tired, and that's saying something. Once we got inside, all any of us felt like doing was sleeping.

By the next morning, all of us were well rested enough that we could start looking for the wolves. We spent most of the day (or what should have been a day) looking for wolves and their tracks. Finally towards the end of the day, we spotted wolf tracks belonging to three different wolves. Yes! I did come to the right place! Hopefully I'll be able to glimpse the owners of the tracks sometime soon. The next day I did glimpse the track's owners. In the forest, I saw a wolf peer around a tree at me and then disappear into the woods. I noticed that that wolf's fur was a bit dark for the wolves living up here. That wasn't the only wolf encounter that I was to have today. Exploring the woods further I found a stream running through the woods. There I found three wolves at the opposite bank. They looked at me and, like the first one, trotted off into the forest.

Over the next week, I caught many glimpses of a wolf pack but I didn't get to see any of their activities. But they seemed to be beginning to ignore me and that was a good sign. The week after, in mid-January, I figured out where their rendezvous site was. After that I saw them more and more often. I figured out that there were six adults in the pack and two half grown pups.

Every day I saw them at their rendezvous site howling, playing or establishing their dominance. There was the alpha pair, the beta male which I recognized as the wolf with the darker coat, two subordinates and the omega. I've seen them make several unsuccessful hunts and hopefully I'll see them bring down a large animal sooner or later.

Fortunately, it wasn't long before I did see them on a successful hunt. It all began at the rendezvous site, which was a hill overlooking the stream. The alpha female stood on the hill and threw back her head and howled. Soon answering cries came from the rest of the pack. Before long the whole pack had assembled on the hill. Once the entire pack had gathered they left in pursuit of prey. This time the pups joined them. Soon the wolves had arrived at a nearby meadow. In the meadow there were about ten caribou. One individual looked very weak. It was limping and lagging behind at the back of the group. I knew the wolves would go for that one. Then the beta wolf broke cover and dashed out towards the caribou. The rest of the pack followed. The caribou immediately broke into a full sprint. The other caribou looked very healthy and ran faster than the wolves. But the straggler couldn't keep up and it became separated from the rest. I saw the beta wolf come around in front of it. The rest of the pack surrounded the injured animal. It had nowhere to run and it was too weak to fight. The wolves easily killed it. All this time the pups had been watching and when the animal was killed they immediately came down to wait their turn to eat. What an experience!

Over the next month or so, we saw the wolves often. In mid-March I was actually lucky enough to witness another hunt. This hunt started out exactly the same way but now that the sun was starting to rise again I was able to see more of it. They even went to the same meadow where there was a group of caribou. I couldn't pick out any individuals that the wolves were likely to go for. The beta wolf slowly approached them before beginning the chase.

Predictably, the caribou ran for it. The wolves chased them into the forest. I still wasn't sure which one they were after. However, they were able to separate one from the herd. They chased it towards the forest. Right before it entered the woods, it seemed to slow down to decide the best route to take through the trees. That was all the wolves needed to catch up. They harassed it and bit at its legs as they chased it through the woods. Finally, back at the rendezvous site, the alpha female was able to tackle it and force it to the ground. Within a few minutes, the animal was dead.

Mid-March is a very important time for the pack—it is breeding season. The alpha male and female seem to be taking a lot of interest in each other. They spent a lot of time together and often took long walks with each other.

Writing to Explore: Discovering Adventure in the Research Paper, 3–8 by David Somoza and Peter Lourie. Copyright © 2010. Stenhouse Publishers.

By the end of the month breeding season was over and things went back to normal. Hopefully I'll be able to see puppies!

By mid-April the sun stopped setting. That meant that I'd be able to observe the wolves at any time. By now the high temperature was 32 degrees and the low temperature was 10 degrees. By late April the stream was beginning to thaw. By early May, the ice was beginning to break up. At that point the alpha female was becoming restless. She began to dig her den in the hill. There the puppies would be born. A week later the den was finished and she would no longer allow any wolves to peer in at her. This was a sign that the birth of the pups was to be any time now. Now the only time the female left the den was to drink and to eat the food the pack brought for her. One day while the female was drinking, the alpha male snuck into the den. When he came out he was gently holding a newborn wolf pup in his mouth. He put it down outside the den and began to lick it. The rest of the pack gathered around the pup to see it. Wolves just love puppies! However, when the alpha female returned, she was furious and she chased the rest of the pack away from her offspring which she brought back to the den.

It is now the end of the month and temperatures are much warmer. The average high is 53 degrees and the average low is 33 degrees. By now the pups are two weeks old and are beginning to peek their heads out of the den. At that point I figured out that there are four puppies. The other wolves in the pack show great interest in them. Soon June arrives and the temperature grows even warmer. They are now three weeks old and are beginning to explore the outside of the den. They are now being weaned of their diet of milk and beginning to eat regurgitated meat. They are very fun to watch because they are now playing at dominating each other. Just one week later the pups are four weeks old and exploring the rendezvous site. The other wolves in the pack truly adore them.

It has to be said that the wolf puppies are just plain adorable! It's hard to believe that in just a week I'll be flying home. It's been wonderful watching the puppies grow up and I hate to leave.

On my plane home to Albany I remember the year I spent with the wolves in Alaska. I have learned many things about them that I could never have learned from school or from books. It's been wonderful being in Alaska, home to the last true wilderness in the United States. I hope my research will help people better understand these magnificent animals. As for the dogs, I think they enjoyed this trip as much as I did, and that's definitely saying something. I know that one day I'll return to this land, the kingdom of the wild wolf.

Writing to Explore: Discovering Adventure in the Research Paper, 3–8 by David Somoza and Peter Lourie. Copyright © 2010. Stenhouse Publishers.

Klara's Bibliography

Web Sites

"Alaska." Late updated April 22, 2006. <www.classbrain.com/artstate/publish>.

"Alaska" Netstate. Last Modified: June 2nd, 2005. <http//www.netstate.com/states/index.html>.

NIST and USNO, The Official U.S Time, Alaska Time Zone. <http://www.time.gov/>.

"Driving Directions Albany, New York to Juneau, Alaska." MapQuest, 2006. <http://www.mapquest.com>.

"Alaska." Map Maker. <http://nationalatlas.gov/natlas/Natlasstart.asp>.

"America The Beautiful–Alaska" Grolier Last Updated: 2006. <http://auth.grolier.com/cgi-bin/authV2?bffs=N>.

"Alaska's Inter-Island Ferry Authority." Southern Route Schedule. Last updated 04/20/06. <http://www.interislandferry.com>.

Prince of Wales Chamber of Commerce. <info@princeofwalescoc.org>.

Prince of Wales Chamber of Commerce. Last updated 12/04/05. <http://www.princeofwalescoc.org/climate.htm>.

American Airlines. Flight Search. <http://www.aa.com>.

Yahoo! Inc. Yahoo! Farechase. Last updated 2006. <http://www.farechase.yahoo.com>.

Uhler, John William. Denali National Park. 1995–2006. <http://denali.national-park.com>.

"Prince of Whales Island Welcome To The Last Frontier" AlaskaGenWeb. <http://www.usroots.org/~princeak/>.

Metz.<contact@princeofwalesonline.com>. Welcome to Prince of Wales Online. Last modified 2006. <http://www.princeofwalesonline.com/reservations.htm>.

<http://www.fs.fed.us/r10/tongass> Last modified: 9/2/05.

Uhler, John William. Gates of the Arctic National Park Last modified: 2003. <http://www.gates.of.the.artic.national-park.com>.

Books

Busch, Robert. *The Wolf Almanac.* Guilford, Connecticut: The Lyons Press, 1998.

Heinrichs, Ann. *America the Beautiful Alaska.* Chicago: Children's Press, Inc.

Whitt, Chris. *Wolves: Life in the Pack.* New York City, New York: Sterling Publishing Co., Inc.

Writing to Explore: Discovering Adventure in the Research Paper, 3–8 by David Somoza and Peter Lourie. Copyright © 2010. Stenhouse Publishers.

Bibliography

General References

Anaya, Rudolfo. 1999. *Bless Me, Ultima.* New York: Warner Books.

Bryson, Bill. 2002. *A Walk in the Woods.* New York: Anchor.

Childs, Craig. 2007. *House of Rain: Tracking a Vanished Civilization Across the American Southwest.* Boston: Little, Brown.

Claytor, Tom. "Tom Claytor Bush Pilot Archive Page." http://claytor.com/archive/15net.html.

Dickens, Charles. 2004. *A Christmas Carol.* New York: Simon & Schuster. (Orig. pub. 1843.)

Hemingway, Ernest. 2003. *Islands in the Stream.* New York: Scribner. (Orig. pub. 1970.)

Lourie, Peter. 1999. *Rio Grande: From the Rocky Mountains to the Gulf of Mexico.* Honesdale, PA: Boyds Mills.

———. 2000a. *The Lost Treasure of Captain Kidd.* Honesdale, PA: Boyds Mills.

———. 2000b. *Mississippi River: A Journey Down the Father of Waters.* Honesdale, PA: Boyds Mills.

Shukman, Henry. 2008. *The Lost City.* New York: Knopf.

Titles by Peter Lourie

Whaling Season: A Year in the Life of an Arctic Whale Scientist. Boston: Houghton Mifflin, 2009.

On the Texas Trail of Cabeza de Vaca. Honesdale, PA: Boyds Mills, 2008.

Arctic Thaw: People of the Whale in a Changing Climate. Honesdale, PA: Boyds Mills, 2007.

The Lost World of the Anasazi: Exploring the Mysteries of Chaco Canyon. Honesdale, PA: Boyds Mills, 2007.

First Dive to Shark Dive. Honesdale, PA: Boyds Mills, 2006.

Hidden World of the Aztec. Honesdale, PA: Boyds Mills, 2006.

The Mystery of the Maya: Uncovering the Lost City of Palenque. Honesdale, PA: Boyds Mills, 2004.

Tierra del Fuego: A Journey to the End of the Earth. Honesdale, PA: Boyds Mills, 2004.

Lost Treasure of the Inca. Honesdale, PA: Boyds Mills, 2002.

On the Trail of Lewis and Clark: A Journey up the Missouri River. Honesdale, PA: Boyds Mills, 2002.

On the Trail of Sacagawea. Honesdale, PA: Boyds Mills, 2001.

The Lost Treasure of Captain Kidd. [Children's novel.] Honesdale, PA: Boyds Mills, 2000.

Mississippi River: A Journey down the Father of Waters. Honesdale, PA: Boyds Mills, 2000.

Rio Grande: From the Rocky Mountains to the Gulf of Mexico. Honesdale, PA: Boyds Mills, 1999.

Erie Canal: Canoeing America's Great Waterway. Honesdale, PA: Boyds Mills, 1997.

River of Mountains: A Canoe Journey down the Hudson. [Nonfiction for adults.] Syracuse, NY: Syracuse University Press, 1995.

Everglades: Buffalo Tiger and the River of Grass. Honesdale, PA: Boyds Mills, 1994.

Yukon River: An Adventure to the Gold Fields of the Klondike. Honesdale, PA: Boyds Mills, 1994.

Hudson River: An Adventure from the Mountains to the Sea. Honesdale, PA: Boyds Mills, 1992.

Amazon: A Journey Through the Last Frontier. Honesdale, PA: Boyds Mills, 1991.

Sweat of the Sun, Tears of the Moon: A Chronicle of an Incan Treasure. [Nonfiction for adults.] New York: Atheneum, 1991. (Paperback published by University of Nebraska Press, 1998.)